X-Ray
Agnivores

Books by Pat Anderson

NOVELS
The McGlinchy Code
The Crimes of Miss Jane Goldie
Torrent
A Toast to Charlie Hanrahan
Catalyst

THE NEO-GERS SAGA
Clash of the Agnivores
Never Mind the Zombies
Rattus Agnivoricus
Damned Agnivores
Another Agnivore in a Different Kitchen
A Trip to Agnivoreville
Hell of the Voidoids
X-Ray Agnivores

FACTUAL
Fear and Smear
Up to Our Knees
Get Over It
The Boattum Line (by Billy 'Burger' King)
The People
Jesus Was A Protestant

FOR CHILDREN
The Skyscraper Rocket Ship
The Ceremony at Goreb Ridge
The Brain Thing
The Football Star
Mighty Pete and the School Bully School

X-Ray Agnivores

THE ERSATZ 55

Pat Anderson

Snowy Publications MMXXI

Copyright © 2021 Pat Anderson

All rights reserved.

ISBN: 9798545534685

To absent friends:

Mick, of Bampots Utd, whose support made all this possible.

Shaun, who first suggested I write these books.

Contents

Preface ix
Introduction xi
1. Art-I-Ficial 1
2. Let's Submerge 14
3. Germ Free Adolescents 26
4. I Live Off You 47
5. Party 59
6. I Am A Poseur 81
7. Obsessed With You 102
8. I Can't Do Anything 113
9. Conscious Consumer 123
10. The Day The World Turned Day-Glo. 133
Notes 139

Preface

All good things must come to an end and so it is with this book series. We had eight years of fun at The People's expense, but we should have guessed that the Establishment would make sure that their team would win the league sooner or later. They certainly picked the ideal time. Celtic was going for ten league titles in a row and there was no way the Establishment were going to allow that to happen.

In my recounting of the past season, there are a couple of things that I decided not to include. The first is the fire-bombing of Peter Lawwell's car, which caused a blaze that could have killed him and his family. The problem with ascribing blame for this incident to The People, or disgruntled Celtic supporters for that matter, is that it wasn't the only incident of this type. Over the past year or so, luxury cars have been attacked in this way throughout South Lanarkshire. The attack on Peter Lawwell's car obviously went wrong. In all other respects, though, it's the same as all the rest.

The second thing I've missed out is the business with Leigh Griffith allegedly requesting pictures from a young girl. It's hard to believe that the Scottish media were telling the truth about the incident; after all, they've been caught lying on numerous other occasions. The police found that no criminal act had been committed, but that's not been enough for some folk. At Celtic's friendly against West Ham United Griffiths was booed when he came onto the pitch. Others applauded, trying to drown out the boos, and the whole thing ended up in a huge argument. It's not an argument I want to get involved in. We don't know the full facts anyway.

You've probably noticed that this volume is a bit thinner than the other books in the series. If you've been reading my blog, you'll know that I had a bit of difficulty writing this book due to my depression. If there's anything I've unintentionally missed out, I'm sure you'll find it in your heart to forgive me.

Anyway, here it is, the last book in the Neo-Gers Saga. Hope you enjoy it and thanks for the support over the years!

Pat Anderson
July 2021

You'll find my blog here:

https://paddyontherailway.wordpress.com/

Follow me on Twitter:

@PatAndrsptr

Introduction
I Am A Cliché

When we left Neo-Gers at the end of the last book, they were still seething about the league being called early and Celtic winning their second Nine-in-a-Row. You might remember that the Ibrox club never argued for the season to be restarted; they simply wanted the league declared null and void. They didn't care about winning the league; denying Celtic the title was their only concern. Despite all their claims of 'dossiers' and the like, however, their quest failed miserably.

Also failing miserably was the annual attempt to sell El Guffalo. The media made their usual sterling efforts on Neo-Gers' behalf, with stories galore about top clubs being interested and even trying to sign him. These desperate attempts to make it look as if Morelos was the object of a bidding war by top European teams hadn't worked before and didn't work this time either. Did they really expect to drum up interest from other clubs by this method? They were obviously as delusional as The People.

Phil Mac Giolla Bhain and his Rugger Guy were still continually looking at Neo-Gers' finances, but hardly anybody was listening anymore. You've got to feel a bit for Phil, he's like a modern-day Cassandra, telling the truth to all and sundry but nobody believes him. In fact, he's usually right about the sad financial state of Neo-Gers, but here they were, still going after eight years. As he constantly mentions, the Scottish media and the Scottish football authorities aren't interested in looking at what's going on at Ibrox. Neo-Gers have become the new Establishment club and they consequently get away with murder.

Clarence the Cross-Eyed Liar aka Honest Dave had departed the scene, so there'd be no more loans coming from that quarter. That was left to Douglas Park and his cronies to take care of. The thing is that buying new players was all very well, but they had to be paid, along with all the other players already there. And that was on top of utility bills, wages for backroom staff and divers other expenses that football clubs incur. The board's bank accounts weren't bottomless pits, so where was the money coming from?

Nobody said it explicitly, but there was a general feeling in the air that this was Neo-Gers' last chance. The truth was that they were skint. They had been living off fumes for years and it simply couldn't go on. They needed the chance to get at the riches of the Champions League and the best way to do that was to win the league title. They were going to need more than a little help in that respect.

Scotland's referees, of course, had always been there to aid the team most of them obviously supported. Even referees that were not Huns, like Willie Collum, had been brought to heel and were terrified of not doing the Ibrox club a favour or two. But, as the last four seasons had shown, the help of the referees wasn't going to be enough. More was going to be needed. Much more.

Meanwhile, The People were complaining about Castore, both the delays in getting the new tops and the poor condition of the tops when they finally arrived. Club 1872 even put out a statement about it.[1] There was also a persistent rumour that Mike Ashley was mixed up with the Castore boys.[2] But then, Honest Dave wouldn't lie to his People, would he?

This was another reason why Neo-Gers simply *had* to win the league this season. If The People were to see Celtic win ten in a row, as well as their 52nd title, they might just give up altogether. It would be like the early 1980s all over again, with hardly anyone going to Ibrox (once they were able to). The People would be unlikely either to buy replica shirts, especially since they already considered them to be not worth the money.

It wasn't all doom and gloom at Ibrox, however. They actually won a trophy during the close season. It wasn't exactly a prestigious trophy, but French teams Lyon and Nice were involved as was Celtic. These other three teams played the matches in the spirit in which they were intended, as friendlies and good training sessions. Neo-Gers, on the other hand, went all-out to win and did. The Daily Record called it 'silverware,' but it looked as if it was made of something other than metal. In fact, it looked like a giant slinky.[3] Still, as Chris Sutton said, they could put it 'next to the Petroltank Cup'![4]

Just like every year, The People were looking forward to yet another season and, just like every year, they were convinced that they were going to win the league this time around. Steven Gerrard felt somewhat differently. He knew that he *had* to win the league if he was still going to be in a job this time next year. He had got a reprieve with the way the season had finished early. If it had continued to a proper conclusion, he'd have been out on his arse. The coming season was his last chance.

The new season was going to be like no other. For one thing, supporters wouldn't be allowed to attend. There were also going to be all manners of rules and regulations to keep Coronavirus at bay. Not the least of these was that clubs would have to test their players at least once a week and only players showing negative results would be allowed to play. The Scottish Government emphasised how strictly these protocols were to be enforced.

> Any failure to adhere to the agreed testing protocol will risk removal by the SG [Scottish government] of the approval for the dispensation given to Premiership clubs compared to the general public in Scotland.[5]

That might seem unequivocal, but it wasn't. It wasn't entirely clear if not adhering to the testing protocol would mean the 'dispensation' being removed just from the guilty club or from *all* Premiership clubs. There was also a little matter that might possibly be construed as a loophole.

> These tests are not carried out by the Scottish government but by private laboratories contracted by the clubs.[6]

That was very nearly a licence for corruption. It was possible that any club that wasn't averse to a bit of cheating could easily finagle the results of the tests. All it would take would be a wee backhander here, a wee misplaced swab there and nobody would be any the wiser. It was a good job there weren't any cheating football clubs in Scotland that would take advantage of such a situation, eh?

Back in May, it was shown in Austria what could happen if football clubs didn't adhere to the rules around Coronavirus. The Austrian football authorities were planning to finish off the 2019-2020 season in June, so teams were allowed to have training in May. Training, however, was only supposed to take place in small groups. The league leaders, LASK Linz, broke the rules by having whole team training. They apologised, using the excuse that they thought it would be okay because all their players had continually tested negative. Ignorance of the law is no excuse, though, and the club was fined €75,000 and docked six points.[7]

If you thought that the same punishments would apply here, then you'd be wrong. Actually, you'd be partly right. This was Scotland and being held accountable and then being punished for it all depended on the club involved. Three clubs were accused of not following protocol in July and Hibs, Motherwell and Neo-Gers were called to the SFA to explain themselves. Hibs had had to cancel a friendly against Ross County at the last minute because their test results hadn't arrived yet. Some of the County team had already arrived at the East Lothian training ground for the match, while others had been informed and had to await further news in Perth.[8] To say Ross County weren't too happy about it is an understatement.

The Motherwell and Neo-Gers situations were slightly different. Both teams had agreed to play a friendly at Ibrox with a six o'clock kick-off. Neither team's test results had arrived back yet, meaning the start time had to be delayed for two hours. It didn't really inconvenience anybody since no supporters were allowed in. The only ones left waiting, apart from the players themselves, were those settling down to watch the game on television.

The three teams received no punishment from the SFA. After all, it wasn't *their* fault that the testing companies had taken so long to get back to them. A warning, though, was given to Hibs since their players had only been tested twenty-four hours before the match with Ross County was due to take place. There was another concern that arose, however, with Neo-Gers. It turned out that they actually *had* broken protocol.

A few hours before the match with Motherwell was due to take place, Neo-Gers fielded a B team against a Dundee United team of the same calibre. The match took place at Auchenhowie/Murray Park/The Hummel Training Centre/Whatever the hell it's called now. The referee was allowed in, but his assistants were refused entry because they didn't have up-to-date verification that they were free of Covid. Since it was a B fixture, the rules permitted the match to be officiated by just the referee. It turned out the two assistants had used the same testing facility as the Motherwell team.[9]

But wait a wee minute here, said everybody, including the SFA. Weren't Neo-Gers awaiting test results as well? Why was it that they had to hang about until eight o'clock before they could play Motherwell, yet they could throw on a full team against Dundee United? Actually, some of the team playing that afternoon did have up-to-date test results. Nine of them, however, had only arrived back from France the day before. Those nine players were Calvin Bassey, Greg Docherty, Andy Firth, Jordan Jones, Ross McCrorie, Glenn Middleton, Greg Stewart, Lewis Mayo and Nathan Patterson.[10] A couple of those names were to crop up again later in the season, especially Patterson.

Now, no club could be blamed for test results turning up late but fielding players without those test results was a different matter entirely. The players could have put the lives of their teammates at risk, not to mention those of the Dundee United players and even the referee. It was worse than what LASK Linz had done, a lot worse. In fact, it was worse than anything any club did before or since. Surely no excuse would be acceptable and Neo-Gers' one that there was a 'misunderstanding of protocol'[11] certainly shouldn't have been. Remember, as LASK Linz had discovered, ignorance of the law is no excuse.

You'll also remember, though, as stated above, this is Scotland. It came as no surprise to learn that the SFA *did* accept Neo-Gers' excuse, flimsy as it was. As somebody from the SFA told the Daily Record,

> Yes, Rangers (sic) should have been well aware of the rules but in the circumstances it does seem as if there was some confusion.[12]

What circumstances were those? As usual, when it comes to Neo-Gers, no details were forthcoming. Essentially, what the SFA was saying to Neo-Gers was that nobody was going to look too closely at anything going on at Ibrox. Our esteemed football authorities would
simply believe any story that Neo-Gers were prepared to tell them. The lesson wasn't lost on Neo-Gers.

So, who was going to help the Widow's Son? Well, the football authorities had already shown willing by ignoring the blatant flouting of Covid regulations by Neo-Gers. There were others too that were ready to lend a hand. As we shall see, there were to be one or two surprises among those helpers.

X-Ray Agnivores

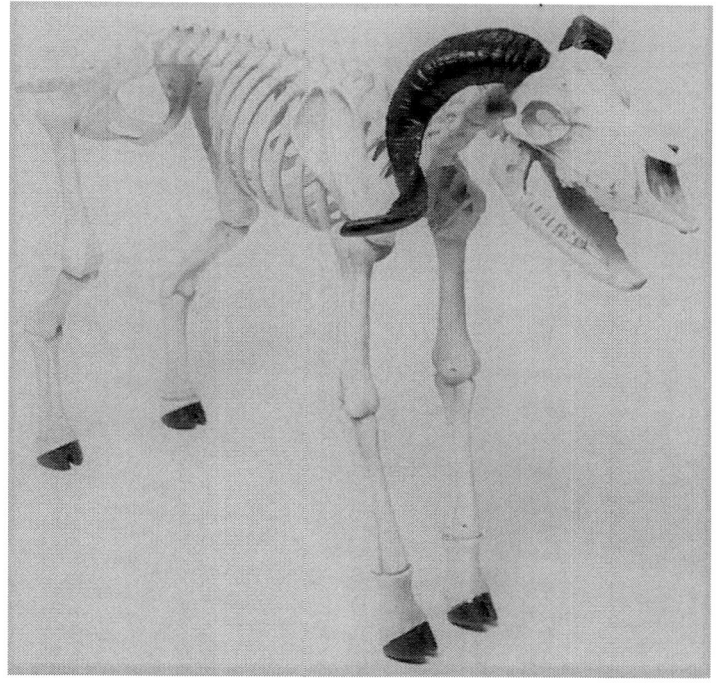

"An' thur stull ridin' mae, even though Ah'm iz deid iz Rangers!"

1
Art-I-Ficial

Neo-Gers kicked off their league season with a 1-0 win at Pittodrie. Steven Gerrard claimed that his side had lain down a 'marker',[1] though it wasn't much of one considering the score. It seemed even less of a 'marker' a day later when Celtic beat Hamilton 5-1, with Odsonne Edouard scoring a hat-trick.[2] In fact it looked more like Celtic were laying down a marker that they were going to win their tenth title on the trot.

There was one marker laid down at Pittodrie, one set by the referee, Brother Boabby Madden. It was getting near the end of the match and Aberdeen were looking threatening around the Neo-Gers box. Neo-Gers managed to get the ball out of their own area to Scott Arfield when in came Andrew Considine to take the ball back. It was a sliding tackle and it's clear that he got the ball, but Arfield went down, holding his shin. Brother Boabby had the red card out immediately and Considine was sent off.[3] Yes, Considine's studs were up, but, as long as the player's done no harm, it's usually a yellow card at most. But this was against Neo-Gers and the opposition was looking threatening. The sending-off was beneficial to Neo-Gers. It wouldn't be the last bit of help from the man in the middle.

Amazingly, Neo-Gers didn't get their first penalty of the season until nearly the end of September. It was a matter of urgency that prompted it. After seven games without a goal against them, Neo-Gers drew 2-2 with Hibs.[4] It also meant that Neo-Gers were only one point ahead of Celtic, who had a game in hand. Steven Gerrard said that he was not panicking just yet;[5] others, however, saw things differently.

Brother Boabby was back in charge a week later when Neo-Gers travelled to Fir Park to take on Motherwell. Neo-Gers were awarded a penalty before the quarter-hour mark for a Motherwell handball. Another came barely twenty-five minutes later, sending Neo-Gers in at the half-time break winning 3-0. Two more goals

1

in the second half made Neo-Gers the 5-1 winners. Motherwell's solitary goal was an Edmundson own goal, meaning that the home side had made no impact at all.[6] The raw statistics, though, don't tell the full story.

Sportscene analysed the penalties, with Michael Stewart opining that they shouldn't have been given at all. This, of course, incurred the wrath of The People, who called Stewart 'biased', 'a bigot' and, as they usually do, brought up the subject of child abuse.[7] They also questioned if Stewart and the rest actually knew the rules.

> They are clear penalties under the current rules. Of course, expecting those imbeciles on Sportscene to actually know the current rules of the sport they are paid to talk about is another matter.[8]
>
> They are penalties under the new rules introduced! They really are fucking idiots![9]

Obviously, the *Sportscene* pundits weren't familiar with the part of the SFA rulebook that specified the separate rules when refereeing Neo-Gers! Sometimes, it's better to go with what one said oneself about a match:

> Actually, from what I could see, Motherwell should have had at least three penalties, and that's not counting the ball hitting a Neo-Gers' players arm just before their fifth goal. One player was cynically scythed down as he made his way into the box, while another was booted on the back of the leg as he prepared to shoot. Stewart pointed out that none of the Motherwell players claimed too much or kicked up a fuss, but, obviously, they knew they wouldn't get any joy out of Brother Boabby.[10]

The BBC wheeled out Hugh Dallas on *Sportsound* to back Brother Boabby's decisions.[11] With his track record, though, you wouldn't expect anything else. He had nothing to say about the penalties denied to Motherwell but, presumably, he thought that his fellow Freemason got those calls right as well.

Another member of The People pointed out that even discounting the penalties, Neo-Gers would still have won the match 3-1.[12] Things, however, aren't that simple. When a team's players are aware that the referee is biased and ready to give their opponents every decision going, the heads go down and they make far more mistakes than they normally would have done. It's an aspect of football that pundits never consider.

After that, it seemed that every time Neo-Gers were struggling in a match a penalty was awarded. An example was the match against Ross County at Ibrox on the 4th of October. Neo-Gers were not playing well at all. As James Tavernier put it, 'We got the three points, but we were disappointed with the performance.'[13] Those three points came courtesy of a 2-0 win. Unsurprisingly, the first of those two goals was a penalty, given on the seventeenth-minute mark.

The same happened when Neo-Gers faced Kilmarnock at Rugby Park. Neo-Gers struggled yet again to find a way past the opposition's defence. As usual, though, the referee, this time Dallas Junior, came to the rescue. It was another handball, and quite a clear one when you see the replay. That replay, however, is a close-up and it's doubtful that Dallas was able to see the incident from the distance and angle he was standing at. The linesman didn't signal at all, obviously seeing nothing. Also obvious is that Dallas simply reacted to the Neo-Gers players claims, doing what was expected of him.[14] Neo-Gers made no further impact on Kilmarnock, winning solely due to that penalty.[15]

Even when Neo-Gers were winning comfortably, it was felt that they needed a penalty. In the next league game after that one at Rugby Park, Neo-Gers were already beating Hamilton 7-0 when they were awarded a penalty.[16] It was the same the following week when Aberdeen came to Ibrox. Neo-Gers were winning 3-0 when Nick Walsh pointed to the spot in the 53rd minute.[17] Perhaps the idea was to give Tavernier a wee bit of extra practice for the next time his services were required.

As well as Neo-Gers getting more than their fair share of penalties, their opponents got none whatsoever, right up until the third week in April, when it no longer mattered. There were times when those opponents should have had penalties, but the match officials made sure they didn't get them. Hibs visited Ibrox on Boxing Day and were beaten 1-0.[18] Hibs player, Joe Newell, was convinced that he should have had a penalty and the height of Hagi's foot certainly supports his claim.[19] Meanwhile, Jim Goodwin, manager of St Mirren, called on referees to be 'brave' when it came to fouls in the Neo-Gers' penalty box.[20] Bravery, though, wasn't an issue; it looked as if there was a fix going on.

The press wheeled out ex-referees to 'prove' that the officials in Neo-Gers matches were making the right decisions. One of these 'experts' supported Willie Collum in not giving Newell a penalty. At best, he argued, it was dangerous play and Hibs should have been awarded an indirect free kick.[21] The fact is, though, that Hibs didn't even get that and Hagi wasn't shown a card of either colour.[22] Actually, that was another thing that went the way of Neo-Gers; they went a whole season without being shown a red card by a Scottish referee.

To the agnivores, it was a sign that discipline had improved at Neo-Gers. Steven Gerrard agreed wholeheartedly.

> In terms of discipline, we're a lot closer now to how we've always wanted it to look. We've always known what we wanted.
> We're representing a club with tradition. Rangers (sic) are a classy club that is all about standards from top to bottom.
> As a group, we were responsible for not having the right discipline. It's something that we've worked ever so hard to improve.[23]

There were various things wrong in that little speech, but it showed that Gerrard had pretty low standards and he was either naively delusional or cynically disingenuous. He made this statement just before the game at Tannadice on the 13th of December. During the match, El Guffalo was shown a yellow card for deliberately elbowing a Dundee United player in the face.[24] To most observers, it should have been a red. Gerrard, however, thought differently, saying, 'I didn't see an elbow.'[25]

The Neo-Gers website, meanwhile, didn't even mention the incident.[26]

Everyone, except for Steven Gerrard, expected the SFA's Compliance Officer to take further action over the incident.[27] Sure enough, El Guffalo was handed a two-game ban, which Neo-Gers decided to accept without complaint.[28] They obviously knew they didn't have a leg to stand on, despite Gerrard's original scepticism.

This became a common theme in Neo-Gers matches; perpetrators of thuggery were either ignored or shown a yellow card. If elements of the media were to highlight these fouls, the SFA would step in with a punishment after the fact. Neo-Gers, of course, complained about these retrospective punishments but, as many on social media were quick to point out, they worked in the Ibrox team's favour.

The truth was that not once, in the whole season, did Neo-Gers' opponents get the luxury of playing against ten men. Neo-Gers, on the other hand, were given this advantage on quite a few occasions. Aberdeen (twice), Hamilton, St Johnstone and Celtic had players on the wrong end of a red card when playing Neo-Gers, benefitting the Ibrox team enormously. Even when an opposition player was sent off ten minutes from the end it was usually when the team was beginning to make inroads on the Neo-Gers goal. It tended to happen too when Neo-Gers' lead was slim or when the score was tied.

Such was the case in January when Celtic visited Ibrox for the second Glasgow Derby of the season. All through the first half, Celtic attacked the Neo-Gers goal but to no avail. Allan McGregor made some spectacular saves, and the Celtic players made some spectacular misses. There were only thirty minutes left to play and the score was still 0-0 when things turned dramatically in Neo-Gers' favour. Of course, it was the referee, Brother Boabby, that provided the turning point. Nir Bitton hauled El Guffalo to the ground, with the Neo-Gers player going down remarkably easily. Brother Boabby had the red card out immediately and Bitton was sent off. Against ten men, Neo-Gers had more of a chance, and they won the match courtesy of a Callum McGregor own goal.[29]

Neil Lennon was furious, claiming that Bitton's foul didn't merit a red card.[30] The media, of course, disagreed. To them, Bitton was the last man and El Guffalo had been denied a clear goal-scoring opportunity. The fact was, though, that Morelos was a good distance from the Celtic goal area and was almost at the touchline. As Lennon said, Morelos might have tried a shot, but it would have been from a very tight angle.[31] It's also the case that other Celtic players were in line with Bitton and Morelos and were charging into the box to head El Guffalo off.[32] Neil Lennon was right; it wasn't a red-card offence. Brother Boabby was just doing his duty by helping the Widow's Son.

The match was also notable for the unedifying spectacle of Brother Boabby holding El Guffalo to stop him getting into more trouble. The thug had already slapped Scott Brown in the mouth; an action which, ordinarily, merits a red card. Not for Morelos, though. Madden was like a teacher holding back a child that's trying to fight with another. If ever there was evidence of Brother Boabby's partiality, it was right there.

As for the business of Neo-Gers players being disciplined after matches were over, Steven Gerrard was forever moaning about it to the media. In February, he told Neo-Gers TV that all he wanted was 'consistency'.[33] This tirade came in the wake of El Guffalo receiving yet another ban, one of three games, for stamping on Ryan Porteous's knee as the Hibs player was on the ground.[34] Gerrard admitted that Neo-Gers had no grounds to appeal the decision, but still moaned like hell. His call for 'consistency' was purely based on the old Ibrox cry of whatabootery.[35]

It should have been other clubs that were calling for consistency, as they saw their players sent off for far less than the likes of El Guffalo was getting away with. If Gerrard had been in any way serious about consistency, he'd have been calling for referees to do a bloody better job. But then, his team wouldn't have an advantage during the match, would they? It's worth pointing out that after Morelos got away with his assault, he scored the only goal of the match. A three-game ban was fair exchange for three points.

El Guffalo wasn't the only thug in blue that benefited from the referees' decisions. Kemar Roofe, who replaced Morelos during his suspension, also got away with murder on the pitch. Just the evening after Gerrard's call for consistency, Roofe was guilty of an assault on a St Johnstone player. Everyone tried to make excuses for him,[36] but it's clear that there was no mistake involved in his lunge.[37] It's also obvious from Roofe's reaction to the yellow card he was shown that he knew he deserved a red.

Surprisingly, Neo-Gers appealed when Roofe received a retrospective two-game ban and were incensed when that appeal was thrown out. As well as reiterating his whatabootery excuse, Gerrard also claimed that the word of referees should be trusted, saying that they did a 'terrific job'.[38] The Daily Record, of course, agreed with Gerrard, calling Roofe's attack a 'mistimed lunge' and speaking of 'trial by TV'.[39] Nobody, however, demanded that the referees be more consistent and diminish the need for retrospective punishments.

It is beyond doubt that match officials played a major part in Neo-Gers' league win. The extent of this influence is debatable; as discussed earlier, wrong and unfair refereeing decisions can have a negative effect on the team at the receiving end. Even when Neo-Gers won by more than one goal the referee's dodgy decisions were there, hanging in the background like a bad smell. We'll never know what could have happened in these circumstances, but we can look at the times when Neo-Gers won by only one goal. This happened on quite a few occasions and in some of them the referee definitely had a hand in the result.

We've already seen how a dodgy penalty helped Neo-Gers win at Rugby Park and how Neo-Gers should have been down to ten men at Tannadice. Meanwhile, Hagi was allowed to stay on the field to score after dangerous play against Hibs at Ibrox and Bitton was sent off at Ibrox to give Neo-Gers the advantage of an extra man. Then there was the incident at Easter Road when El Guffalo was permitted to keep playing after stamping on a Hibs player. He later scored the only goal of the match. And there was Roofe's assault on a St Johnstone player in February, when he was only shown a yellow card.

On top of all that, there was the game at Pittodrie in January, which Neo-Gers won 2-1. Neo-Gers were awarded a penalty when the score was still 0-0. There didn't look to be any contact when El Guffalo went down and if there was it was purely accidental.[40] There is a rule nowadays, commonly known as 'double jeopardy,' which says that a penalty is punishment enough and there's no need to send off the offender, which would be a double punishment. That contact was accidental, if there were any, made the sending off even more harsh. The Daily Record tried to justify the referee's decision[41] but the fact that the referee's name was John Beaton tells you all you need to know.

The opposing teams might well have won these matches if it weren't for the cheating referees, but let's be generous to Neo-Gers and say they'd have been draws. That means that they got two points in each of those games that they shouldn't have. That's fourteen points they were handed courtesy of dodgy refereeing. It certainly makes the huge points margin that Neo-Gers won the league by a lot less impressive.

Even after the league had been clinched, the cheating went on. The reason was that Neo-Gers were looking to claim the title of 'Invincibles,' matching 'Brendan Rodgers' Celtic side of 2016-17,' as the BBC put it.[42] That was going to be pretty hard to do. In that season, Celtic were unbeaten in all three domestic competitions; Neo-Gers, meanwhile, had already been knocked out of the League Cup. Still, it wouldn't be the first time that delusion played a part in the Neo-Gers story. Anyway, the agnivores were all excited about Neo-Gers going the whole league campaign unbeaten, and the referees were ready to lend a helping hand.

The first match after Neo-Gers won the league was at Celtic Park. Celtic were winning 1-0 when Odsonne Edouard was scythed down in the Neo-Gers box. It was a stick-on penalty but the referee, Willie Collum, decided instead to book Edouard for diving.[43] Collum's card had been marked a couple of years previously and he wasn't going to stick his neck out and be the first to award a penalty against Neo-Gers. That honour was left to another.

There was a bit of cheating in the game against Hibs at Ibrox, with a Hibs goal disallowed for no reason that anyone could see. Apparently, there was a foul, but nobody could make out exactly who had fouled whom. If anything, it was a rather pathetic dive.[44] The really obvious bit of help, though, came in the next game at Perth against St Johnstone.

St Johnstone had been a hard team to play against throughout the season, winning the League Cup and the Scottish Cup. On the 21st of April Neo-Gers had cause to find out just how tough the Perth team could be. They couldn't make any inroads against the dogged St Johnstone and had to do some dogged defending of their own against a team that was determined to get something out of the game. It took until nearly the hour mark before Neo-Gers managed to score and they then had to try to keep St Johnstone from scoring an equaliser. Then St Johnstone were awarded a penalty.

It was something you could see coming a mile off after Neo-Gers won the league. For years, back when Rangers were still alive, we were always told, when it came to the Ibrox club getting more than its fair share of penalties, that 'these things even out over the season'. It was a lie then and it's still a lie when they try to use the same story to justify the penalties Neo-Gers get. This was what the penalty awarded to St Johnstone was all about. But things had to be done right.

The referee, Euan Anderson, didn't point to the spot immediately. He at first signalled for a goal kick and then changed his mind and awarded the penalty. He was doing what he'd been told but thought he'd better check with the linesman. Whether the linesman was higher up in the Ludge, or whether he was in contact with somebody that was, Anderson was told to change his mind again.[45] It was all very well giving St Johnstone a penalty but, with about twenty-five minutes left to play, there was every chance that they'd go on and win the match. How the hell would Anderson explain away destroying Neo-Gers' 'Invincibles' record? And on the Queen's birthday too!

Anderson finally got his chance to award that penalty when it was safe to do so; well into injury time in the 95th minute.[46] And very relieved and satisfied he looked too![47] The job had been done. The old lie about 'things evening themselves out' was still in place and Neo-Gers' 'record' was secure. Anderson had saved the day, himself and his position in the Ludge.

When Celtic were knocked out of the League Cup by Ross County,[48] it must have seemed to Neo-Gers that all their Christmases had come at once. Here was the chance of a double, or even a treble. Conversely, a huge groan must have gone up in Paisley when St Mirren were drawn against Neo-Gers in the Quarter Finals.[49] That groan would have been even louder when they discovered that Andrew Dallas would be the referee.[50] Their last two games against Neo-Gers with this character in charge had hardly endeared them to him.

The first of said matches was in February 2019. That was the notorious occasion on which Dallas gave Neo-Gers *four* penalties.[51] Some teams don't even get that many in a whole season! The next time the two teams met with Dallas in charge was in August 2020. St Mirren knew they'd get nothing out of the game no matter what and, accordingly, played quite nervily, being beaten 3-0.[52] The result of the upcoming match seemed a foregone conclusion.

It was a matter of intense relief, then, to the St Mirren players when Dallas, while warming up, pulled up with an injury. We don't know exactly what was wrong with him, but he'd probably aggravated an old groin strain he'd got from shagging goats down the Ludge. At any rate, he had to pull out (of the match, not the goat) and the fourth official, David Dickinson, stood in as referee. Dickinson didn't have much experience at top level, but he was a qualified referee; the Real Deal, so to speak. And, since he wasn't one of the more well-known names, he was probably cheap as chips as well. (Sorry, couldn't resist!)

Because Dickinson had never refereed in the top tier (as far as we know), nobody had bothered yet to give him a copy of the special rule book about taking charge of Neo-Gers matches. He consequently did several things he wasn't supposed to, like not sending off a St Mirren player when he got the chance. Bongani Zungu got a set of studs in the ankle, but Dickinson only showed a yellow to the perpetrator. He also committed the unforgivable sin of giving a penalty against Neo-Gers when they were winning 1-0.[53]

St Mirren scored from the spot and this rare occurrence rattled Neo-Gers, allowing St Mirren to score again and take the lead. It was near the end of the match that Dickinson made his final error. Steven Davis managed to get an equaliser in the 88th minute. It looked as if extra time was on the cards, which, obviously, would have suited Neo-Gers, giving them a quick breather and a chance to reorganise. With that in mind, any other referee would have blown the whistle as soon as possible. Dickinson, however, decided to play injury time.

St Mirren scored in the 92nd minute, giving The People and Masons everywhere apoplexy. All was not lost, though. Brother Boabby or Cheatin' Beaton would have kept the game going until Neo-Gers scored. Dickinson, however, blew the whistle two minutes later.[54] Neo-Gers were out of the League Cup. Dickinson was no doubt drummed out of the Ludge the very next evening and was never heard of again. Rumours that he's buried in somebody's back garden in Harthill have yet to be confirmed.

Matt McGinn wrote a song called *Footba' Referee*, in which he described refereeing a match between Rangers and Celtic. He sang,

> The half o' them said, He's a Fenian wi' a heart to Ireland
> The others said, He's a blue-nose and he's had the shake o' the hand.[55]

While it's true that both Celtic supporters and The People believe that referees have it in for their respective teams, statistics don't lie and it's obvious that both Ibrox teams, old and new, have always got far more than their fair share of decisions going their way. There's also the matter of the evident allegiances of Scottish referees. Has anybody ever heard of an ex-referee speaking at a Celtic function, joking that he made sure Rangers never had a chance? Or what about a referee being an ex-season-ticket holder at Celtic Park? Or a referee being pictured drinking, and celebrating, at a Celtic pub?

Alan Muir is a different beast entirely. Over the years, he's incensed everyone from Chris Sutton[56] to The People.[57] Although he's often been accused of being biased,[58] the fact is that he's simply incompetent. He used to officiate at UEFA matches until he was removed from the FIFA list in 2011.[59] I can't find any reason for his removal, but I'd imagine it's because he was bloody useless. Essentially, he shouldn't be in charge of a schools' football match, let alone one in the top tier. He obviously has friends in the right places.

Having friends in the right places, though, wasn't enough. He'd shown that he wasn't up to refereeing on the international stage, but this was Scotland. As long as he made sure that Neo-Gers won, nobody would care how incompetent he was. Nobody that mattered anyway. Surely he couldn't make an arse of that!

This is the man that was put in charge of the Scottish Cup Quarter-Final between Neo-Gers and St Johnstone. He was probably given instructions on how to handle the game beforehand, but he couldn't even get that right. The People, with their usual sense of entitlement, expected Muir to play along, as their post-match complaints indicate.

> I honestly cannot believe how we are reffed to a different standard in every game we play.[60]

> Because the referees operate under the auspice of a corrupt organisation.[61]

> If we had committed the fouls St Johnstone committed, we'd have had two straight reds and one off for a second yellow.[62]

This from a supporter of a club that hadn't seen a red card in a domestic game all season! The People were so used to getting either a penalty or two or an opposition player sent off that, when it didn't happen, they automatically assumed that the referee was biased against their team. Their ridiculous lack of awareness continued:

> Because for years our Club has sat back and taken bad and corrupt decisions against us, mainly without any complaint.

> And when we have complained, it's been all rather half-hearted tbh.[63]

This character obviously forgot how Neo-Gers got Willie Collum banned from officiating their matches until he learned to toe the line!

Anyway, with no dodgy penalties or sending-offs to rely on, Neo-Gers simply had to play the match the way it's meant to be played. The game ended in a 0-0 draw, which necessitated extra time. Even then, St Johnstone held their own and the final score was 1-1. And so, it was a penalty shoot-out, something that should have worked in Neo-Gers' favour. After all, which other team in Scotland have had so much practice at taking spot kicks?

As it turned out, though, St Johnstone won 4-2 in the penalty shoot-out.[64] Incredibly, James Tavernier was the first to take a penalty for Neo-Gers and had it saved by Zander Clark. Borna Barisic and Jermain Defoe both scored for Neo-Gers' second and third, before Kemar Roofe's shot was saved, meaning St Johnstone, who had scored with all three penalties, only needed one more to win. Alistair McCann stood up to the pressure and scored, sending St Johnstone through to the Semi-Finals.[65]

Both the cup quarter finals against St Mirren and St Johnstone proved one thing: Neo-Gers were a bang average team, who'd have got nowhere without the help of match officials. Indeed, if it hadn't been for the referees, Neo-Gers would have struggled to be in the top six. But cheating referees were only a part of how Neo-Gers were helped by Scotland's football authorities. If the rules had been properly applied, Neo-Gers might well have been candidates for relegation, instead of winning their first league title.

2
Let's Submerge

In April 2021, twelve European clubs, including six from England's Premier League, announced plans to form a Super League to rival the Champions League.[1] Matches would be played in midweek so as not to interfere with domestic leagues. Amid all the talk of this new league being for the benefit of football as a whole, it soon became clear that it was solely for the financial benefit of those twelve clubs, plus another three that were expected to join.[2]

Understandably, many were angry at this idea, which would effectively be a closed shop, with only five other clubs allowed to take part on merit. Everybody in England was dead against the idea, including Boris Johnson, the FA and even the fans of the clubs involved. Probably the main concern of the FA was the sheer embarrassment of the possibility of teams in the middle of the Premier League qualifying for the Champions League while the top six buggered off to the new Super League. UEFA, as you might guess, were dead set against the whole idea; not least because attention began to be focused on their own competition.

In many ways there was not a lot of difference between the Champions League and the proposed Super League. For one thing, the Champions League was a misnomer. It wasn't a competition for champions; far from it. The same rich clubs seemed to take part year after year, whether they were champions of their domestic leagues or not. England, for example, sent its top four teams straight into the competition every year. The champions of Scotland, meanwhile, had to navigate through various qualifiers to get into the league stage. A seeding system was used to keep the so-called top teams apart, meaning that the same clubs invariably appeared in the knock-out stages. Then there were UEFA's rules and regulations.

A few teams have fallen foul of the rules about ineligible players over the years, but other rules were not so stringently applied. There were supposed to be strict regulations concerning Financial Fair Play, but the richest teams were able to bypass these without too much trouble. These rules were there to stop clubs spending money they didn't have, which could lead to ruin, not just for the clubs concerned, but to European football overall. Some clubs, however, were certainly *not* living within their means. Predictably, those teams were the ones looking to set up the new Super League.

Not only were these teams not living within their means, but they had run up a combined debt that even an African despot would be embarrassed at.[3] So what happened to the FFP regulations? It looked as if some clubs were more equal than others! UEFA then proposed changes to the Champions League, along with the Europa, but these appeared to just involve increased prize money, to the benefit of the usual crew.[4]

With financial irregularities so evident at the top level of European football and FIFA being a by-word for corruption,[5] it's hardly surprising that Scotland's football authorities are of the same ilk. The figures might seem laughable next to those of the top tiers in England and Europe, but everything is relative. In football terms, Scotland is a financial backwater, with prize pots measured in seven or eight figures,[6] rather than the ten-figure sums splashed out on English football by TV companies.[7] And Scotland's record payment for a player, the £12m squandered by Rangers on Tore Andre Flo,[8] looks like very small beer next to the £198m paid by Paris Saint-Germain for Neymar.[9]

That £12m spent on Tore Andre Flo happened in 2000 and helped contribute to the massive (in Scottish football terms) debts that killed Rangers. The new Ibrox club, however, didn't learn from the old club's mistakes and, almost from its inception, Neo-Gers have run at a loss every year. By November 2020, Neo-Gers' cumulative debts since 2012 have been an astonishing eighty-odd million quid. Even some top European clubs would baulk at that figure!

Although The People would argue the point, Neo-Gers, by dint of coming from Scotland, are one of the minnows of European football. (The same could be said of Celtic, of course!) As such, they're open to being subject to FFP rules, unlike Barcelona, Real Madrid etc. They've managed to get around these regulations by continually converting their loans, from members of the board, into shares. This has worked so far, but it goes without saying that this way of working is hardly sustainable.

Since Honest Dave's Masonic Hall Putsch in 2015, Neo-Gers have relied on loans from him and his cronies just to keep the lights on. At least, that's been the story, but Honest Dave is not known for using his own money for anything and the details of transactions are pretty murky. People that know a lot more about these things than I do seem to be convinced that something decidedly dodgy is going on.[10] The problem is that Neo-Gers shares aren't dealt in any exchange at all, meaning that it's hard to keep track of who's bought what. It suits Neo-Gers to work under these arcane methods.

Since Neo-Gers shares aren't traded on an exchange, it also means that there's no way of knowing how much they're worth. The shares can only be traded privately and are only worth what a buyer is prepared to pay for them. All the stuff about shares being worth 20p each is a load of nonsense. It doesn't take an economist or an accountant to realise that the more share issues there are, the less each share is worth. As many have pointed out online, there have been so many issues that they can no longer be worth much. In fact, they're probably not even worth the paper they're printed on.

Any computers at Ibrox will have been long ago sold off and photocopiers are too dear for Neo-Gers' fly-by-night operations. One price I've seen is 0.8p for each A4 photocopy,[11] which is probably more than double what a share is worth. No doubt share certificates are churned out on an old Banda machine they picked up on Freecycle. At any rate, Neo-Gers shares are practically worthless, but there are still those stupid enough to buy them. Step forward The People.

If you remember, Honest Dave stepped down from his post as chairman in March 2020, leaving Douglas Park in charge. In December, he announced that he was selling his shares, which supposedly numbered over 66 million. The 'lucky' recipients were going to be Club 1872, who were going to have to fork out over £13m for the privilege. He said,

> My all-in cost is 23.7p per share and I am willing to put a pricing structure in place that accommodates 20p as the initial price to be consistent with the present share issue.
> And, at Club 1872's request, I have included an option for Club 1872 to buy all of the shares at 20p which would result in a loss to me. In my view the shares are presently worth in excess of 50p if properly valued.[12]

The shares, however, couldn't be properly valued because they weren't being openly traded on a stock exchange. King, a convicted fraudster, was just plucking figures out of the air. How the hell could the shares be worth more than double their initial price when more and more shares were being churned out on a regular basis? And King was hardly known for his philanthropic nature so it's doubtful that he was selling at a loss, as he claimed. Perhaps that figure of 50p he came up with was the total cost of those 65 million shares! At any rate, The People were being conned and, being the thick creatures they are, were perfectly willing to believe everything Honest Dave told them.

As well as conning The People over share prices, Honest Dave, aka Clarence the Cross-Eyed Liar, also grossly overstated how much Neo-Gers players were worth. According to him, the players were worth about £200m altogether.[13] Quite how he reached that figure only he knows, but The People, gullible as ever, were ready to believe every word. After all, they've been bandying about inflated prices for El Guffalo for years now.

It was around the same time as King's bullish claims that Neo-Gers' managing director, Stewart 'Hullo Hullo'

Robertson admitted that the club was going to have to sell a couple of players come the summer. He showed much the same delusion as Honest Dave, saying that any bid for a player would have to be worthwhile.

> It has to reflect our valuation. And if that is the case, we'll have a decision to make.
> While player trading is the important fourth pillar to our model, we have not got ourselves in a position where we have to sell to validate the model. That's not the case.[14]

The big problem with that was that the only ones believing Neo-Gers' valuations of their players were The People and the agnivores. Normal folk have eyes and minds of their own, with which they can easily see that Neo-Gers players are pretty average and rely on match officials to see them through. The agnivores have been trying to flog El Guffalo for years, with little to no interest shown despite all their stories to the contrary. James Tavernier, meanwhile, is being touted as worth a fortune by Neo-Gers,[15] although anyone with any sense can see that his impressive goal tally has mostly come from penalties. Like Neo-Gers shares, the players are only worth what somebody is willing to pay for them. Neo-Gers would have to find another method of raising revenue. And revenue they most definitely need.

All those people suing the new club haven't just vanished into thin air. They've been twiddling their thumbs, patiently awaiting the end of the Covid pandemic so the courts can open again. From Mike Ashley to the firm that was contracted to build a memorial garden, there are plenty of folk just waiting their turn to take Neo-Gers to the cleaners. I doubt any of them would be prepared to accept poorly-printed share certificates in lieu of hard cash! And there was yet another court case pending that, although not directly affecting Neo-Gers, went to the very heart of the Big Lie.

It took BDO, the liquidators of Rangers, long enough to realise that Duff and Phelps had possibly acted fraudulently in their backstairs deal with Charles Green. The arguments had been going back and forth since 2017, but it was 2021 before there was talk of a court case actually going ahead. With the pandemic still around, though, there was no sign of a date for any hearing.

Duff and Phelps, of course, contested all allegations. A spokesman said,

> Basically what they allege is that we should have shut the club down.
> They allege that if we closed it down we would have got more by selling Ibrox and then selling the playing squad and we say that is nonsense.
> They say we should have broken up the heritable assets and sold the playing squad, even though Craig Whyte couldn't sell any of them other than Nikica Jelavic during the transfer window and we are supposed to sell them outside of the transfer window.
> Do they really think that's a viable strategy? It's just bonkers.[16]

What was 'bonkers' was administrators selling off assets at all instead of doing what they were supposed to do: find a buyer for the club as a going concern. Duff and Phelps argued that BDO's strategy of selling assets to the highest bidder would have 'effectively shut the club down for good.'[17] That immediately begs the question: what about it? Duff and Phelps were supposed to be acting in the interests of the creditors, not the club. When nobody was willing to buy Rangers, the whole lot should have been handed over to the liquidators.

BDO apparently had Ibrox valued and found it was worth £25m.[18] As we saw above, Duff and Phelps dispute this and stand by their actions in selling practically everything to Charles Green. Of course, the Big Lie makes it seem as if the administrators did their job properly and sold Rangers as a going concern to Chateau Charlie. They didn't give a damn about the creditors and left nothing for the liquidators other than a pile of debts. If the good folk at BDO had had their wits about them, they'd have challenged the dodgy deal with Green there and then, instead of waiting until it was possibly too late.

Although The People tend to avoid using the dreaded 'L' word, they sometimes mention liquidation when they're looking for somebody to blame. A myth has grown that claims that the liquidation of Rangers was completely unnecessary.[19] This requires holding two completely antithetical opinions at the same time; that 'cognitive dissonance' that Phil Mac Giolla Bhain always goes on about. On the one hand, they believe that Green and everyone else around at that time was 'bad tae Raynjurz,' while on the other they believe that Green and his cronies 'saved Raynjurz.' No wonder they're always so violent!

The same cognitive dissonance was shown by the Freemasons in Police Scotland. Everyone involved in the dodgy sale of Rangers' assets was rounded up and arrested. So angry were the rozzers at these alleged fraudsters that there were stories of them singing *The Billy Boys* as they questioned the administrators.[20] Whether by sheer incompetence or by design (that cognitive dissonance at work, not wanting to hurt the ones that saved Raynjurz) the coppers buggered up the whole operation. The whole sorry mess was thrown out of court, the Judge Advocate agreeing with Tory politicians that an independent inquiry was needed into this 'malicious prosecution'.[21]

As usual, when it comes to an Ibrox team, the public purse is left to pick up the tab. Police Scotland and the Crown Office were both being sued by various characters that had been unsuccessfully prosecuted in this major guddle. The compensation figures being bandied about were utterly ridiculous, reaching eight figures in some cases. Altogether, by May 2021, the figure had reached £113m and was expected to rise.[22] It boggles the mind how such amounts can be justified, especially when you consider that the Guildford Four only received £500,000 each after fifteen years in prison for something they didn't do.[23] Even allowing for inflation, that figure still comes in at less than a million quid,[24] while the lads at Duff and Phelps are getting several million each.

At any rate, this farce can't have done much for BDO's case. Imagine trying to pursue folk through a justice system that's already made a complete arse of prosecuting those selfsame folk! It looks as if the Big Lie is safe; for another while at least.

We've strayed a bit from the subject here, which is the Ibrox finances. Considering what we've already looked at, it's understandable that the boys in the Blue Room aren't too keen on anybody questioning where the money's coming from. One commenter that did, Andy Walker, found himself banned from Ibrox. He had said, on Sky Sports News, that Neo-Gers were in a 'perilous financial situation'.[25] Of course, Neo-Gers took umbrage at that, and Walker was soon absent from the Sky commentating panel when they were at Ibrox. Then again, maybe Neo-Gers simply ran out of soup!

It was no wonder Neo-Gers were determined to cover up the truth. With all the companies queuing up to take money from them and the club's debts climbing year after year, it was easy to see that the 2020-21 season was make-or-break for Neo-Gers. The club desperately needed the chance to get at the possible riches of the Champions League with all the TV money and gate receipts that go along with it. There were other considerations as well.

It can't have escaped anyone's notice that there were far more Neo-Gers tops about in May 2021 than usual. Thousands of fair-weather fans forked out for Neo-Gers shirts after the team had won the league. Meanwhile, all manner of tat was available for purchase to celebrate what they were calling their fifty-fifth league trophy. It appeared that it was now a matter of pride to support Neo-Gers rather than the embarrassment it had been for the previous decade. But what if Neo-Gers *hadn't* won the league?

Away back at the beginning of the season, The People were moaning like hell about the Castore replica shirts.[26] Apparently, none of the logos were sewn on and some of them weren't even ironed-on transfers. There were instances of stickers being slapped onto generic tops, while any transfers were of dabbity quality at best. They would probably disintegrate in the wash, which made it fortunate that The

People rarely bathe let alone do laundry. God only knows how the shoddy tops would react to the rain!

With The People having such a poor opinion of Neo-Gers tops, they would hardly be persuaded to part with their hard signed-on-for cash if Neo-Gers failed, yet again, to win any trophies. The rest of the rubbish available from the online Neo-Gers store would also be left to rot in the depot. The physical shops, meanwhile, would soon be having closing-down sales, with nobody there to snap up the bargains. Season ticket sales would drop, and The People would desert their team in droves.

It's happened before. If you're old enough to remember the 1980s you'll know what it was like at Ibrox when John Greig was in charge. They couldn't give season tickets away and anybody that wanted in, which weren't many, could simply pay at the gate. The People are a fickle bunch. They think they're superior beings and can't stand it when their team continually proves them wrong. Celtic winning ten in a row and only being two more titles away from '54' would have them tearing their hair out and refusing to set foot inside Ibrox ever again.

As it turned out, The People would be clamouring for season tickets as soon as they went on sale, as well as forking out for anything with the number 55 on it. No wonder the Establishment pulled out all the stops to ensure their favourite club won the league.

One expected piece of revenue was the £2.8m Neo-Gers felt it was due from its deal with Hummel. Mike Ashley, however, put the kybosh on that particular plan when a judge decided that he was in the right in May 2001.[27] The amount might seem a drop in the ocean compared to what Neo-Gers owes, but every penny counts especially since the club was looking to spend yet again.

Oli McBurnie has hardly been a hit at Sheffield United and has belied the £20m they paid for him by only scoring seven times in two years. He hasn't been a favourite of Scotland's national team's supporters either. In sixteen appearances for the senior side, he's failed to score at all. Actually, that's not strictly true; he scored in the penalty shoot-out against Serbia in November 2020.[28] Needless to say, considering his prowess from the penalty spot, he's a lifelong Hun.

He also happens to be a bit of a thug, as was shown in a video of him attacking folk in the street.[29] He'd fit in well at Ibrox, then; in fact, they'd probably end up having a statue of him outside the stadium. The People have already taken him to their hearts because he's refused to take part in 'huddles' at both Swansea[30] and Sheffield United.[31] (Well, it's a Sellick hing, intit?)

McBurnie, for his part, always wanted to play for Rangers and now wanted to play for Neo-Gers, saying, after meeting Steven Gerrard in Dubai, 'I want to play for him. It's f***ing Stevie G, it's Rangers'.[32] Of course, with Sheffield United being relegated, McBurnie was looking to leave. He was linked with Neo-Gers at the end of May, with him apparently being a target of Steven Gerrard's.[33] Sheffield United, however, will want to recoup some of their money and will be looking for around £15m. Neo-Gers better hope that somebody will pay their inflated price for El Guffalo.[34]

If Neo-Gers do intend spending millions on new players, then they'll have to use whatever financial sources they used throughout season 2020-2021. As mentioned above, secrecy surrounds those sources, whatever they are. All we ever hear about is loans, but, surely, they must be drying up by now. Douglas Park and his ilk don't have unlimited funds and all those worthless shares are hardly compensation. Still, The People are easily gulled.

At the start of June, Neo-Gers announced yet another share issue, from which they hoped to raise £6.75m.[35] It was aimed at both investors and ordinary fans, although how ordinary fans would be able to afford the minimum purchase of £500, they didn't say. The maximum purchase of £100,000 was obviously meant to tempt large investors, though it's doubtful anybody with any sense would want to throw their money away on this basket case. Their best hope would be Club 1872 or other groups of The People pooling their money. They'd be the only ones taken in with all the pish about 'an iconic football club', 'a prestigious 150-year history', invincible 55th titles and the like.[36]

Another seven-figure amount had already been secured, from the Scottish Government of all people! This money had been set aside to help Premiership teams that had lost out on revenue because of Covid regulations. £20m was made available, which meant each club would receive about £1.6m each. This was an interest-free loan, which could be paid back over a period of twenty years, with the first payment not due until 2022. Apparently, one club didn't take up the offer, leaving £1.6m free. This extra cash was given to Neo-Gers, meaning they had a loan of £3.2m.[37] Quite why the Ibrox club has received double what every other club got is a mystery. The mystery is solved somewhat, however, when you discover that the money wasn't given straight to the clubs but was administered by the SFA. Now everything makes sense!

Again, though, this loan money and the money from the share issue wouldn't come anywhere near covering Neo-Gers' debts, let alone allowing the purchase of new players or even paying their wages. And those weren't the only expenditures Neo-Gers were looking at. Edmiston House was going to be demolished to make way for a fan zone and a museum. This was to be completed in time for their 150th anniversary, which should give them a good 141 years to get the project finished. The Big Lie, though, meant that they had about a year to get things ready. A video showed the exciting new building, which would contain a two-storey shop, an event space for conferences, gigs etc. and a museum.[38] The media were calling it the *Temple of Doom*...er...*Dreams*. Shades of casinos and floating pitches there!

As always, Neo-Gers are using the plans as yet another way to fleece The People. They're offering 'Official Supporter Packages for
Edmiston House,' which include 'Your name inscribed on the Official Supporters Wall in the new Rangers (sic) Museum' and...not a lot else, really.[39] Oh, wait, you get a wee model of Ibrox Stadium and the new Edmiston House and 'Priority window to purchase tickets for Rangers (sic) hosted events held in Edmiston House.'[40] Notice it doesn't say *all* events; just those hosted by Neo-Gers, whatever those might be. The price for this fantastic opportunity is 150 quid per person for a

'lifetime package'. A lifetime? Isn't that what they said about the debentures?

That little enterprise wasn't exactly going to bring in millions and neither were the planned flats on the Albion Car Park.[41] Unless Neo-Gers were going into the real estate business, they'd just be getting paid for whatever the car park's worth. It certainly wouldn't cover the cost of demolishing Edmiston House and building and furnishing the Temple of Doom. And that brings us back to where we came in. Where the hell's all the money coming from?

Well, there have certainly been some dodgy characters at Ibrox, including Clarence the Cross-Eyed Liar, who The People think saved them from all the thieves and rogues. And remember when Honest Dave himself admitted that there were folk 'linked to organised crime and money laundering' investing in Neo-Gers?[42] In fact, rumours have abounded for years that money laundering has been going on at Ibrox.[43] There are even stories about the DUP being involved and evidence of some very dodgy dealings occurring.[44]

Of course, with compliant media, football authorities in thrall to Neo-Gers and a police force heavily intertwined with Freemasonry, nobody has been looking into the finances at Ibrox. Anyone stepping out of line and carrying out such an investigation would soon find themselves, at the very least, branded a delusional paranoiac. No wonder Neo-Gers feel secure in continuing with their dodgy finances.

3
Germ Free Adolescents

As already mentioned, Neo-Gers' first game of the new season was at Pittodrie, with 'Brother Boabby' Madden in charge. They beat Aberdeen 1-0, which sounds quite a boring match. The agnivores, however, talked things up, making it seem exciting, although the fact that they reported Aberdeen as having 'little bite' somewhat belies that opinion.[1] The only real talking point in the game, other than the goal, was Aberdeen having a man, Considine, sent off near the end. Actually, there was one other talking point, but that came after the match.

In what might have been a case of drowning their sorrows after the defeat to Neo-Gers, eight Aberdeen players took it upon themselves to go to the *Soul Bar* in the city that Saturday evening. After a meal in the dining area, they retired to the bar proper for a few drinks. Unfortunately for them, somebody took a picture that was soon doing the rounds on social media.[2] Even more unfortunately, two of the players subsequently tested positive for Coronavirus, forcing all of them to self-isolate.[3]

The big question that nobody asked was why a pub-cum-restaurant was open at all. It was open because the Covid rules had been relaxed for a time, with many places, restaurants especially, open to the public. The UK Government encouraged people to use restaurants as much as possible during August to help the ailing economy. They called it *Eat Out to Help Out* and even subsidised restaurants so that they could offer discounts.[4] It could be argued that those Aberdeen players were just doing their civic duty, as they had been encouraged to do by Boris Johnson's government. It was hardly their fault that the Westminster Government's harebrained scheme helped to foster a second wave of Covid infections.[5] Neither was it their fault that Aberdeen had become a Coronavirus hotspot.[6]

These players could have used the excuse of confusion with some justification. Footballers tend not to be the brightest bulbs on the Christmas tree, even at the best of times, so the idea of them being confused about regulations would be perfectly acceptable to the general public. Besides, they weren't the only ones confused about the rules regarding pubs and restaurants. Only one team, however, is allowed to get away with excuses like that so, instead, the eight Aberdeen players issued an abject apology.[7]

The day after everyone read those Aberdeen players spilling their guts, both Celtic and Neo-Gers were in action again. Neo-Gers kicked off against St Mirren at 3 o'clock and won 3-0. St Mirren spent practically the whole match defending in their own half.[8] You could hardly blame the Paisley side for playing in this manner; the referee, Andrew Dallas, would make sure they had no chance of getting anything out of the match.

Celtic played away to Kilmarnock, starting at 4.30. It proved to be a lamentable display from Celtic. Despite exerting constant pressure, they could only manage one goal. That might have been enough to win if Kilmarnock hadn't been awarded a penalty, making the match end up 1-1.[9] It certainly looked as if Jullien hauled the Kilmarnock player down,[10] but, to paraphrase umpteen television and radio pundits, I've seen them *not* given (particularly when a Neo-Gers player does it). As it turned out, however, the papers weren't that interested in Celtic's inability to score or whether it had been a penalty or not. They had a bigger story.

It was in the dying moments of the match that Neil Lennon took off Greg Taylor and replaced him with Boli Bolingoli.[11] It was a like-for-like substitution and was hardly going to make a huge difference to the game. As things turned out, however, it was the most important moment of the match. It was to have far-reaching consequences for Celtic and, as the agnivores argued, possibly for the whole of Scottish football.

As the agnivores fell over themselves to tell us, Bolingoli, unbeknownst to Celtic, had taken a quick trip to Spain in the week before the match. He should have been self-isolating but, instead, kept quiet about his brief holiday, attended training and came on as a substitute with nobody any the wiser. The agnivores, almost gleefully, told us that Bolingoli had been 'putting every player and match official at risk.'[12] Meanwhile, politicians of every hue spoke about the possibility of the season being cancelled only two games in.[13]

Bolingoli issued the customary apology to the media, while Celtic, who were said to be 'furious' and 'raging', hauled the player in and promised
an 'internal probe'.[14] The People, of course, wanted Celtic to be punished as well as Bolingoli.

> Points deduction, nothing less!
> WATP[15]
>
> Celtic and Aberdeen must be closed down sporting integrity demands it.[16]

It had only been about three weeks, but it looked as if The People had already forgotten what their own club had done. The agnivores had, rather conveniently brushed the whole affair under the carpet. Celtic and Aberdeen had done absolutely nothing wrong, but all the anger was focused on them, instead of on a club that had deliberately flouted the rules by knowingly fielding a team with no test results. As usual, though, that particular club was off-limits when it came to criticism.

Nicola Sturgeon was blazing about both Aberdeen and Celtic, demanding that their next few games be postponed.[17] She said, 'Consider today the yellow card. The next time it will be the red card because you will leave us with absolutely no choice.'[18] Aberdeen had already missed a game against St Johnstone; now their matches against Hamilton and Celtic were being postponed. Celtic, meanwhile, as well as that game against Aberdeen, were having the midweek match against St Mirren postponed.[19] It seemed like a strange sort of punishment. Then again, maybe it was just intended to stop any possible spread of Covid.

It certainly wasn't enough for Fatboy Dim, Kris Boyd; he wanted both teams hammered. At first, when it was just Aberdeen involved and their games against Hamilton and Celtic looked like going ahead, he was bleating about 'sporting integrity'. St Johnstone weren't being allowed to benefit from a reduced Aberdeen side, so why should Hamilton and, more importantly, Celtic?[20] (Those eight Aberdeen players that went out on the town were having to self-isolate for two weeks.)

As soon as Celtic were involved, however, Boyd changed his mind dramatically. Now he wanted all those postponed matches cancelled and the points awarded to Celtic's and Aberdeen's opponents. The match between Celtic and Aberdeen should be cancelled outright, and Kilmarnock should be given the points for having to play against a team with an 'ineligible' player. He cited Celtic being reinstated to the Champions League in 2014 when Legia Warsaw had fielded an ineligible player as a precedent.[21]

Nobody in charge followed up Boyd's suggestion, which was hardly surprising. Boyd was too thick to realise that going down the 'ineligible player' route in Scotland might prompt a scrutiny of all those 'improperly registered' players that the old Rangers had fielded down the years. Ironically, Boyd was one of those EBTers, which should, if he had any brains, have led to him keeping his head down and his mouth closed on such a topic.

At any rate, Celtic had two games postponed, while Aberdeen had three. Each club was also fined £30,000, although £22,000 of that was suspended, only to be coughed up if there were any more breaches. The Aberdeen players were given a suspended three-game ban. Bolingoli was immediately banned for three games, with a further two suspended. Celtic, however, had already sent him out on loan.[22]

Boyd would have been cheered to read the *Daily Record's* take on what Celtic's suspended matches meant. With Neo-Gers having three games to play before Celtic kicked a ball in anger again, they had the opportunity to go eleven points clear.[23] Certainly, Celtic would have games in hand, but there is a psychological disadvantage to having to play catch-up. The more paranoid among us would suggest that this disadvantage was the whole point of Celtic's games being postponed. After all, the club had done nothing wrong.

Another aspect of the whole business of these players breaching Covid regulations was one that the media never bothered to broach. This was the fact that there always seemed to be somebody around with a camera. The Bolingoli revelations were especially dodgy. Apparently, a picture of the Celtic player going on his overnight jaunt to Spain was taken by a Celtic supporter, who was later angry when he saw Bolingoli come onto the pitch against Kilmarnock.[24] There was something, though, that didn't quite ring true about this story.

So, a Celtic supporter goes on a plane and sees a Celtic player on the same flight. He makes no effort to communicate with the player or ask him where he's going. Instead, he takes a sneaky photo when the player's not looking. And what does he do with the picture? Apparently, this 'Celtic supporter' thought Bolingoli was going to Spain to talk to a Spanish club about a transfer.[25] Anybody else would have posted the picture on social media, questioning whether the player was leaving or not. Not this character, though. He held onto the picture until he saw Bolingoli take the field against Kilmarnock, which makes you wonder why he took the picture in the first place.

Another thing that's strange is that the guy got in touch with the *Daily Record*, an organ that no Celtic supporter views as a friend. But, then again, *was* his first stop the DR? *The Sun* boasted that it was the one that had broken the story,[26] so the 'Celtic supporter' must have contacted them first. The question is, when? Did he get in touch with them straight away and *The Sun* sat on the story, waiting to inflict maximum damage? Or did *he* wait until it would hurt Celtic the most? In either case, the whole thing stank to high heavens.

Of course, The People imagined that the stink was coming from Parkhead way. One individual, reminiscent of our old chum PZJ, attempted to line up information he got from the police under an FOI request with flight arrival times at Prestwick.[27] Like PZJ, he had no idea what the information meant and made a complete arse of himself. For one thing, he stated that there were no flights from Malaga to Prestwick then goes on to detail the flight from Malaga to Prestwick that Bolingoli supposedly took. He also assumed that Bolingoli would have been issued with a Fixed Penalty as soon as he got off the plane when no crime had been committed yet!

One or two posters on the forum pointed out his errors, but most of them agreed with him wholeheartedly. A couple even added their own embellishments, such as Bolingoli being picked up at the airport by someone from Celtic. A few, though, thought the whole enterprise was ridiculous.

> No offence mate, but do you not have anything better to do with your time fs?[28]

> OP you need a burrd, a dog, or in general something in your life.[29]

> Get a life ffs. Obsession with the opposition is their deal not ours.[30]

The Vanguard Bears, meanwhile, called for a 'Points deduction and heavy fine for Celtic.' Their reasoning was that 'Players lives were in jeopardy.'[31] This echoed Kris Boyd's demands in *The Sun*, where he wanted Celtic punished, citing their 'failure to control their player'. He made it plain that he felt the same way about Aberdeen and stated, 'And I'd be saying the same if it was Rangers (sic).'[32] It wouldn't be too long before those words would be put to the test.

Let's skip to the start of October, when a two-week international break prefaced Neo-Gers' first trip to Celtic Park. At this point, Neo-Gers topped the league with 26 points, with Celtic only 1 point behind with a game in hand.[33] Everything was still to play for as the media built up what they insisted on calling the first 'Old Firm' encounter of the season.

It was a completely brainless idea having international matches in the middle of a pandemic, but money talks in football and UEFA are no exception. Of course, the inevitable happened: players Europe-wide contracted Covid. Clubs with international players in their ranks had to face losing important members of their teams when they had to self-isolate; that included Celtic. Odsonne Edouard tested positive and was stuck in isolation in France.[34] The same happened to Nir Bitton, although he was self-isolating in Glasgow after featuring for Israel against Scotland at Hampden.[35] And those weren't the only ones that wouldn't be able to play against Neo-Gers.

The Scotland team turned up in Edinburgh to train for the match against Israel and were tested for Covid. Southampton and ex-Celtic midfielder Stuart Armstrong tested positive and was put into isolation. Two players, Kieran Tierney and Ryan Christie, were identified as close contacts and also had to go into isolation.[36] Both players had tested negative and Celtic, not to mention Arsenal, were not best pleased.

A rather strange fact was that Armstrong had tested negative on arrival, along with the rest of the squad. It wasn't until the next day, the 6th of October, that he returned a positive result.[37] The strangeness of the episode lay in the assumption that Tierney and Christie, along with a couple of backroom staffers, were the only ones Armstrong had any contact with.

Ironically, Armstrong was available to play for Southampton after isolating for 10 days, although the Saints didn't take any chances and left him out of the squad on the 17th.[38] Tierney and Christie, on the other hand, despite numerous negative tests, were required to stay in isolation.[39] Both players claimed to have conformed to the rules, staying well apart in the hotel room and playing games on different consoles,[40] but nobody was listening. Celtic and Arsenal petitioned strongly to have their players' isolation ended early but to no avail.

The People were clear about what they wanted to happen, as exemplified by this clown in the Daily Record's Hotline:

> Once again Celtic are crying foul on Covid-19 rules which apply to everyone in Scottish Football. The whole Celtic team should be quarantined if Christie has been in contact with someone who tested positive and the Old Firm (sic) game should be postponed with the points awarded to Rangers (sic) as per the rules.[41]

This character doesn't seem to understand the meaning of the word 'postponed'. I think he meant 'cancelled'. Anyway, the Lothian Health Protection Team, the Scottish Government and the SFA suddenly had a change of heart. It seemed that the rules could be bent after all. Unfortunately, this only applied to Kieran Tierney[42] and, sure enough, Tierney turned out for Arsenal that Saturday.[43]

Celtic, of course, assumed that Ryan Christie would be treated the same way; they assumed wrong. No reasons were given for the different treatment, just a glib statement about anyone 'coming in close contact with a person who has tested positive requires the full 14 days of isolation.'[44] It was strange how everybody had to stick to the full letter of the law when it came to a Celtic player. There was a definite Jim Farry-like stench hanging over the whole affair.

Neo-Gers won the match 2-0. Even with those missing players, you'd have expected Celtic to put up a bit more of a fight. They were so bad that they made a bang-average Neo-Gers team look good. Both goals came from set-pieces, which was a worry. Something appeared to be going very wrong at Celtic. That, however, is a subject for another chapter.

On the 1st of November, Neo-Gers beat Kilmarnock 1-0 at Rugby Park. (Again, a subject for another chapter.) Not featuring in that day's game was Scott Arfield, but it was still a special day for him. It was his birthday; he'd reached the ripe, old age of 32. No doubt he watched the match, but he'd have been more excited about getting ready for his birthday party. But, then, that would be illegal, wouldn't it? Under Lockdown restrictions, nobody was allowed to go to other people's houses. You weren't even allowed to visit your granny. Surely a player from a law-abiding organisation like Neo-Gers wouldn't do anything untoward, would he?

Then, on the Monday, it was announced that two Neo-Gers players, George Edmundson and Jordan Jones were among ten people issued with fixed penalty notices when police had to break up a house party in Glasgow's West End.[45] Apparently, Neo-Gers knew all about this before anybody else, which begs the question of who told them. It was doubtful that Edmundson and Jones would have grassed on themselves, meaning that the rozzers must have contacted somebody at Neo-Gers to let them know what had happened.

Both players were immediately put into isolation and were suspended, pending an investigation.[46] It was all done and dusted before noon. Something just didn't smell entirely kosher about the whole thing. There were too many coincidences, for one thing. These two players went to a party on the same day that just happened to be the birthday of one of their colleagues. And then there was the fact that the two were decidedly fringe players so no real harm was done to the team. It all seemed a little too pat.

Speculation was rife on social media that it was all a cover-up; that Arfield *did* have a party, which was attended by several first-team players.[47] Since the police obviously alerted Neo-Gers to the situation, it isn't too much of a stretch to conclude that the officers in attendance were Neo-Gers supporters. This being the case, they'd hardly want to see their team handicapped by the loss of important players. It looked as if Neo-Gers, with the connivance of Glasgow's Finest, decided to throw under the bus two players that were surplus to requirements.

The rumours persisted that it had been Scott Arfield's party and that more players than just this unfortunate pair attended.[48] Some folk even put pictures online, showing El Guffalo and others partying. The People were unimpressed, claiming that the pictures were old ones from Instagram.[49] The media, meanwhile, employed their own countermeasures.

A video emerged, purportedly showing the party that Edmundson and Jones had attended. Strangely, neither of the players appeared. There was a photo, however, claiming to show Edmundson, looking at his phone, apparently in the same flat.[50] That so-called evidence, though, was just as dodgy and inconclusive as the ones being posted online by Celtic supporters. It proved absolutely nothing.

The story being peddled by the press was that Edmundson and Jones met an attractive female online, one of a group staying at a hotel in Glasgow's city centre. Obviously believing there was the prospect of a shag, the players invited the woman and her friends to a party. Instead of having an orgy at one of *their* flats or houses, however, they invited the young women to a party at Devonshire Terrace.[51] It all seemed highly unlikely, but it was the only story we were getting.

Kris Boyd was incensed at Edmundson and Jones, not least because he'd been put in an awkward position. He'd blasted

Celtic and Aberdeen, you'll recall, for not 'controlling' their players. Now, he'd be expected to do the same for Neo-Gers, just like he'd promised he would. Instead, though, he tried desperately to wriggle out of things.

> Let's get it right — this isn't in the same ballpark as the controversial incidents at Celtic and Aberdeen earlier this season.
> Eight lads at Pittodrie went out on the town, while Boli Bolingoli jumped on a plane and flew off to Spain for a break, for crying out loud.
> Jones and Edmundson aren't as bad as that lot[52]

How the hell did he make that out? Neither Celtic nor Aberdeen had been aware of what their players were doing. Was Boyd implying that they had? And the actions of Edmundson and Jones (and maybe others) were actually worse than what those Aberdeen players had done. Remember, at the time those Aberdeen players went 'out on the town' it was perfectly legal. In fact, the UK Government had encouraged the patronising of pubs and restaurants. The Neo-Gers players had no such excuse.

Essentially, Boyd was nothing but a hypocrite, blaming Celtic and Aberdeen for what their players had done, but absolving Neo-Gers of any culpability when the same thing happened to them. His previous calls for Celtic and Aberdeen to be docked points could now be seen exactly for what they were: the raving machinations of a bitter Hun!

The SFA served Jones and Edmundson with a charge, with both of them having to appear at Hampden on the 19th; there was no word, though, of any punishment for Neo-Gers.[53] The pair was hit with a massive seven-match ban when their case came up at Hampden.[54] Of course, it wouldn't make much of a difference to two players that wouldn't have featured in those games anyway. Unlike in the cases of Celtic and Aberdeen, Neo-Gers seemed to have been absolved of any and all responsibility. Nobody was blaming Neo-Gers for 'not controlling their players'; quite the contrary, in fact.

After Nicola Sturgeon's previous performance, going on about yellow cards and the like, everybody expected the Scottish Government to come down hard. Was it time for the 'red card' and Scottish football to be abandoned? Incredibly, the statement from the Scottish Government was nothing of the sort.

> We commend Rangers (sic) for taking such swift and decisive action in this instance, to protect the rest of their squad and wider public.[55]

Er…isn't that what Celtic and Aberdeen did as soon as they became aware of their players' actions? And yet, both clubs were fined, while Neo-Gers got off scot-free. It makes you wonder exactly what the fines were for. It looked as if there was an agenda to help Neo-Gers. The fact that there was no investigation into the full story of the infamous party tends to support this view. Neo-Gers' version of events was accepted without question and the two sacrificial lambs were going to miss games that they wouldn't have featured in anyway. And there wasn't just a pro-Neo-Gers agenda; an anti-Celtic agenda was at work as well.

Every year since 2017, Celtic have gone to Dubai in January, during the winter break, to take advantage of training in warm weather. They're not the only football team to do it and other sports teams take advantage of the top-class facilities as well. The big problem this year was, would it be acceptable or even wise to go to the U.A.E. in the middle of a global pandemic? They were going to have to make sure they got official approval.

You couldn't get much more official than the SFA and the Scottish Government, both of whom gave Celtic permission to go to Dubai back in December.[56] It defies belief that Celtic wouldn't have double-checked that it was still okay before boarding their flight and, as Neil Lennon pointed out, if there had been a problem, why didn't anybody say?[57] At any rate, on Saturday the 2nd of January, Celtic took off for Dubai.

Of course, Celtic could go nowhere, it seemed, without somebody with a camera following them. A picture started doing the rounds, online and in the press, showing Neil Lennon and Scott Brown enjoying a pint by a swimming pool.[58] Another had some Celtic players sitting around a table in a bar.[59] It was just one instance and just one pint, but the way the media went on it was as if the trip to Dubai was nothing but a drink-fuelled orgy.

The press made a huge deal out of the affair, as did several Celtic bloggers. The word 'jolly' was bandied about a lot. It got so bad that Celtic had to post daily pictures on their Twitter account to show that the players *were* actually training.[60] The Scottish Government, meanwhile, called for the SFA to investigate Celtic.[61] It looked as if the SNP was trying to secure the votes of The People, even though it was a fruitless exercise. One blogger had more to say on this subject.

> Apparently, it had been made clear to Govt that if they didn't do everything they could to hamstring Celtic, that come Indy2 the terrorist organisations linked to Ibrox would cause as many social issues as they could.[62]

> Would politicians facilitate that to assist, in any way, their agenda of Independence. Fucking right they would. Know why? Won't stop any of us voting YES. They know that. Won't.stop me. They have a belief that they might get the "Orange vote"... They won't but with OO and UVF contact saying they won't cause too much trouble.......[63]

As the blogger was at pains to point out, he had just heard this from one person, but it made perfect sense. He certainly wasn't alone in thinking along these lines. There was *something* that smelled about the whole thing. Without hard evidence, we could only speculate about what that something was. Neil Lennon had the same kind of thoughts and expressed them in his 'infamous' online media conference.

> Why didn't they (the Scottish Government) stop us from going then? We flew out on the Saturday, the

country went into full lockdown on the Monday. You can't tell me the government didn't know that we were going into full lockdown before we flew out on the Saturday?[64]

It was starting to sound like a put-up job, a way to get Celtic into trouble. And the singular treatment of Celtic continued when the team got back from Dubai. Instead of the 2m rule for keeping your distance, which was known worldwide, Celtic were ordered to maintain a *3m* distance.[65] This was according to Neil Lennon, but hardly anybody was listening. If you look at the comments under the blog I've just cited, it's clear that next to nobody believed what Lennon was saying. One question that was asked was why nobody at Celtic made an official complaint or, at least, backed up what Neil Lennon was saying. The reasons for that will be made clearer later in this book.

Lennon didn't miss many folk out in his online attack and one thing he was particularly incensed about was the way he and his players were being castigated for having a pint while others had been practically encouraged. For example, the Scotland squad had celebrated winning a penalty shoot-out against Serbia to qualify for the Euros by doing a conga to Baccara's *Yes Sir I Can Boogie* and then partying the night away in their hotel.[66] Pictures showed that there was no social distancing observed at all. And yet, there wasn't a word of criticism to be found anywhere. In fact, the celebrations were hailed as 'a sign of the team-spirit under Steve Clarke.'[67] Looked at in light of that little episode, it was clear that Celtic were being treated unfairly.

To the delight of the agnivores, Christopher Julien tested positive for Covid when the team returned from Dubai. The media immediately assumed that he'd picked up the virus over in the UAE; after all, you couldn't expect foreigners, especially Arabs, to adhere to Coronavirus protocol, could you? As was pointed out by bloggers, as well as Neil Lennon, Julien could just as well have picked up the virus if he'd stayed in the UK.[68]

Thirteen first-team players, along with Neil Lennon, John Kennedy and another, unnamed member of staff, were told to self-isolate, despite all having tested negative.[69] As things turned out, another, unnamed, Celtic player tested positive while he was in isolation.[70] This seemed to justify the whole isolation procedure and validate the Scottish Government's treatment of Celtic. There was, however, an element that nobody considered worth investigating.

Although Celtic's, and other teams' players were testing positive for Covid-19, none of them were reported as showing any symptoms. Nobody ended up like that poor sod Derek Draper, husband of TV's Kate Garraway.[71] Surely at least one player should have exhibited signs of infection. But, no; nary a sniffle or a cough was ever reported. Basically, everyone was relying on the testing procedure to tell them who was capable of infecting others. The assumption was that everything connected with Covid testing was above board. But was it?

In November, Channel 4's programme *Dispatches* exposed serious failings in the laboratories in Northern Ireland. The investigation uncovered instances of lax procedures, which could lead to cross-contamination and the tests of 'VIPs' being given precedence, holding up the test results of us lesser mortals.[72] The BBC's *Panorama* found similar faults at a laboratory in England.[73] These stories didn't come as too much of a surprise since the UK Government's whole approach to the Covid crisis had been flawed, to say the least, from the very beginning.

The UK Government's handling of the pandemic, moreover, has been riddled with corruption. Tory donors and pals of senior Tories were given huge contracts dealing with track-and-trace, testing and Personal Protective Equipment (PPE) even when they had no experience in such matters.[74] It's worth reading that whole article I've just referenced to understand the scale of what was happening. With so much corruption going on, who would notice a bit more? A wee contaminated test sample here, a wee change on the results papers there – who would be any the wiser?

This might sound unnecessarily paranoid, but the SFA has a history of corruption, the Jim Farry/Jorge Cadete affair being but one example. With their referees already doing their bit to aid Neo-Gers' prospects, what was one more bit of help going to matter? Of course, neither I nor anyone else has any proof of this and the SFA's obsessive secrecy means that we probably never will. At any rate, what this means is that all those players having to isolate was a way of punishing Celtic without it looking like a punishment.

Around the same time that Celtic were coming back from Dubai, another team was just arriving. It was the Great Britain Olympic Gymnastics Team going to train for the games that had been postponed in 2020.[75] Strangely, nobody found any fault with this; in fact, it was hardly even mentioned in the UK media. It seemed that only Celtic were to be condemned for going abroad.

Every day, flights were going in and out of Britain, albeit on a reduced basis. If the UK Government had been serious about protecting us all from Coronavirus, all the airports should have been closed, all flights cancelled and any plane straying into British airspace should have been blasted out the sky with ack-ack guns. But no, the airlines making money and business deals being concluded were far more important than mere human lives. And flying to and from 'banned' countries was remarkably easy to do. All one had to do was fly to a country that was deemed safe and continue one's journey from there, as Boris Johnson's father did.[76]

While they were in Dubai, nobody followed the Gymnastics Team around with a camera, so there were no photos of what went on. That might well have had something to do with the fact that taking pictures of people without their permission is illegal in Dubai, as Neil Lennon pointed out.[77] But that wasn't the only reason no pictures were taken. Neo-Gers travelled to various matches in Europe but there were no photos of any of their players at their hotels or anywhere else for that matter, apart from when they were taking part in the games. Whether they stuck to the rules or not is immaterial; no other club in Scotland was accorded such respect.

With the sense of entitlement that Ibrox is imbued with from top to bottom, it was only a matter of time before another breach of the regulations occurred. Or, rather, the first breach that we heard of occurred. On Sunday the 14th of February – Administration Day – the news broke that Neo-Gers were 'aware' of online allegations that two, or perhaps even four, players had attended a house party. Neo-Gers announced that they were conducting an 'internal investigation'.[78] Would we actually hear the truth this time and would the *real* perpetrators be punished?

Alex Rae, the man that looks like a lobotomised Jason Statham, advised Neo-Gers to be careful what they did in the run-up to their very first league title. He said,

> First and foremost, if it was key players, you have to protect that asset.
> You have to factor in that if it if is key players you are going for a title and maybe overlook it as opposed to if it was a younger guy and you want to send out a message.[79]

It looked as if Rae was advocating a bit of cheating. He seemed to be implying that Neo-Gers should perhaps throw some younger players under the bus instead of admitting that more important players were involved; assuming they were, that was. When it was announced that five players had been at a party and their names were given, it appeared that Neo-Gers had taken Rae's advice. The players named were Bongani Zungu, Nathan Patterson, Calvin Bassey, Dapo Mebude (who was on loan at Queen of the South) and Brian Kinnear.[80]

All of these players were young, apart from Zungu, who was twenty-eight. Patterson was nineteen, Bassey twenty-one, Mebude nineteen and Brian Kinnear was twenty. It looked like another Jones and Edmundson job to protect the first-team players. All of these characters were surplus to requirements. They might be 'promising', but they weren't needed at present. Even Zungu was at Neo-Gers on loan and no decision had been made yet whether to buy him or not. He was expected to remain and become a first-team regular within a couple of years. None of these players were needed by the first team. Everything, however, was soon to change.

On the 25th of February, Royal Antwerp came to Ibrox to play the second leg of their match in the knockout stage of the Europa Cup. There, on the bench, were Zungu, Patterson and

Bassey. Zungu and Patterson both featured in the match as substitutes.[81] What the hell was going on? The answer could be found in the first leg of the match over in Belgium. It had been an eventful game to say the least, with three penalties and umpteen fouls. The surprising thing was that the referee only handed out six yellow cards and one red.[82] Neo-Gers won the game 4-3 but both Kemar Roofe and James Tavernier were injured and were major doubts for the next week's match.[83]

Neither player was able to feature in the second leg.[84] Gerrard had cover alright but there was still a dilemma; what if anything happened to *them* during the match? Or what if they were having an off day? Others were needed for the bench, so Gerrard turned to three of what came to be known as the Covid Five. Neo-Gers won again, this time 5-2, two of those goals coming courtesy of penalties. But the big question was, should Patterson and Zungu have been playing at all? To add insult to injury, Patterson scored one of the goals.[85]

Gerrard defended his decision to have the three players on the bench by saying that they were being treated no differently from Edmundson and Jones. They had had to self-isolate, had been fined and had been suspended from the club.[86] Presumably, those suspensions ran concurrently with the self-isolations, which in Patterson and Co's case was ten days. There was, however, a problem with that explanation that, of course, nobody in the media bothered to point out.

Gerrard didn't name the Covid Five until the 17th of February, after the so-called 'internal investigation.'[87] Now, if that was when they were told to isolate, then their ten days wouldn't have been up until the 26th – the day *after* that game against Antwerp. But let's give them the benefit of the doubt and say that they went straight into isolation on the 15th, the day after the party. That would fit since they would have been able to go back to training on the 24th. They would, however, have missed nearly two weeks of training; would one day before the match be enough? Unless, of course, they had been training along with their teammates and the story about self-isolating was just a ruse.

Furthermore, since we're assuming that the players self-isolated after they'd been caught by the police, wouldn't either they or some friendly copper phone Ibrox and let them know the score? That makes the story of an internal investigation a complete load of Craig Whyte. Perhaps the rumours of a cover-up were true;[88] not that our esteemed Fourth Estate would ever investigate that! Whatever really happened, there was a whiff of deceit around the whole business.

When Gerrard announced the names of the rule breakers, he also stated that Neo-Gers were 'in dialogue with the SFA and the Government moving forward to find the solution in terms of those boys.'[89] Since the club was in talks with the powers-that-be, those powers would have been well aware of the problems facing Gerrard

with regard to injury. He was going to need Patterson, Bassey and Zungu for domestic league games as well as in Europe.

If you remember, it took the SFA less than a month to dish out punishments to Bolingoli and the Aberdeen Eight.[90] The same was true of the Neo-Gers fall guys, Edmundson and Jones.[91] For this latest breach, the SFA took a full six weeks to reach a decision about punishments.[92] There was no reason at all for taking that long about it, which points to it being solely about helping Neo-Gers. No excuses were given for the delay. None were needed since the SFA was quite blatant about their agenda by this time.

In a brazenly shameless display, Neo-Gers almost immediately appealed the bans handed out to the five players, which were four matches with another two suspended.[93] Yet again the SFA was cravenly compliant. The date set for hearing the appeal was the 20th of April, giving Neo-Gers at least another week to field the three players still at Ibrox.[94] The league, of course, was over by this time but there was still the Scottish Cup to play for. With Tavernier still out injured, Gerrard needed Patterson in his squad at the very least. It was a cynical move by Neo-Gers, supported to the hilt by the SFA. It was nothing short of disgraceful.

By the 6th of March Neo-Gers were 18 points ahead of Celtic and on course to win their first ever title or, as the agnivores would have it, their first title in ten years.[95] They were due to play St Mirren at Ibrox, and a win would bring them within 1 point of the title. The People decided to get their celebrations in early and turned up at Ibrox to welcome the team. Covid regulations were still in force but The People, as usual, were a law unto themselves. None of them wore masks as they crowded together, many of them had children with them and various smoke bombs and fireworks were set off. Meanwhile, the police stood by and watched.[96]

Neo-Gers won the game 3-0, making the league competition all but over.[97] With the title within their grasp, it was time for The People and their team to celebrate. Pyrotechnics went off outside, while the team ran to the gate to greet the supporters.[98] Then, it was party time. Music blared in the changing room as the booze flowed.[99] The agnivores were in celebratory mood as well, showing happy pictures of El Guffalo at the changing-room window holding a bottle of beer.[100] They didn't, however, show everything that happened.

Pictures showed supporters leaning in the changing-room window to celebrate with the players, while, apparently, children were passed through the window to mix with their heroes.[101] When the players left it was five to a car, no masks and windows open to allow supporters to get up close and personal.[102] The whole team should have had to isolate, but not a word was said about it by anyone in the SFA, the police or the Scottish Government. It seemed that Neo-Gers were above the law.

By the time of Neo-Gers' final game of the season there was no longer any 'seemed' about it, it was definite; the law simply didn't apply to Neo-Gers. After the team was presented with the League Trophy, it was party time. They all gathered in a bar within Ibrox Stadium, where the drink flowed, and the music blared.[103] (We'll deal with the sectarian singing later.) There were a few short videos knocking about of the celebrations, but nobody, least of all in the Scottish media, had anything to say about Covid regulations being broken yet again.

The infamous video of the Neo-Gers players celebrating has something interesting going on at the right-hand side.[104] If you ignore the singing and concentrate when the video moves to the right, you will see a member of staff stopping someone from recording the scene on his phone. That's a member of the bar staff, not a member of Neo-Gers' backroom team.

Another video (which I can't locate) showed a female member of the bar staff interacting with El Guffalo. Unless the bar staff had been locked away since the previous March, it showed a clear breach of Covid rules. That, however, wasn't the worst of it.

Another video showed James Tavernier, Connor Goldson and Nathan Patterson turning up at a house with the League Trophy and then joining in a party. The video was apparently sent to the Daily Record, who ran with the story and then, almost immediately, removed it.[105] Unfortunately, MSN weren't informed of the change of heart and the original Daily Record story was available there.[106] Meanwhile, folk on Twitter had made screenshots of the original article and uploaded them. There were plenty of videos showing the party as well.[107]

Nathan Patterson, you might remember, had already received a four-match ban for breaking Covid rules and there was a two-match suspended ban to be enforced if he broke the rules again. Well, here he was breaking them again, but we heard nothing about any ban. In fact, he was picked for the Scotland Euros squad with not a word said about him breaching regulations. The police claimed to be investigating the incident, but we heard nothing more about it. No doubt we never would hear anything more about it.

And so, Neo-Gers ended their season the same way they'd started it, by running roughshod over Covid regulations with impunity. They had fielded a team against Dundee United that didn't have any test results away back in July and now they were mixing with the public and destroying the 'bubble' they were meant to be in. No other team in Scotland would have got away with such flagrant flouting of the rules. There was, though, another aspect of the celebrations after the win against St Mirren; something that nobody paid any attention to.

Sports people are a notoriously superstitious lot. They all have 'lucky' pieces of clothing or pieces of jewellery that they feel they can't compete without. Then there are the little rituals that they perform – making the sign of the cross, kissing their hand and then touching the pitch or track or whatever. Some go through long, elaborate performances reminiscent of voodoo rituals. One thing that they all have in common is that they don't like tempting fate by celebrating before everything's done-and-dusted.

Football teams are usually banned from jumping the gun, even when they're only one game, or one point, away from success. It makes the scenes in the Ibrox changing room on the 6th of March all the more striking. There was always the chance that Neo-Gers might lose all their remaining six games, while Celtic won theirs. Why did Gerrard let his team celebrate prematurely? Did he know something that the rest of us didn't?

4
I Live Off You

Ever since the days of Fergus McCann, Celtic have shown an almost pathological fear of debt. You can hardly blame them. Most of us still remember those days in 1994 when Celtic almost went bankrupt and the utter glee with which our esteemed Fourth Estate greeted the news. Luckily, The Bunnet came to the rescue and a share issue was enthusiastically taken up by Celtic supporters everywhere.[1] McCann, though, instituted a severe fiscal policy, which, at the time saw demonstrations against him. He refused to sign the players Celtic might need to stop Rangers' inexorable march toward equaling the Parkhead club's record of nine titles in a row.

It took until well into the new century for McCann's policies to make sense. By that time, Gavin Masterton, David Murray's sugar daddy,[2] was long gone from the Bank of Scotland and Lloyd's, who now owned the bank, wanted their money. We all know what happened then; Rangers were put into liquidation and died. In retrospect, Celtic supporters realised that McCann had been right all along. And if Celtic were to go the way of Rangers, you could be damn sure that nobody would be allowed to start a new club and call it 'Celtic'!

For the last decade or so, Celtic have settled into a policy of buying young players cheaply, developing them and then selling them on.[3] It seemed a worthwhile fiscal scheme, but it was hardly what you'd call ambitious. Remember, that UEFA Cup final in Seville was the result of Celtic spending some money on already-established players for a change: the likes of Chris Sutton and John Hartson. There was also Henrik Larsson, who stayed at Celtic for seven years. That would never happen these days with a player of his calibre.

Since those halcyon days, Celtic have hardly shone on the European stage, and no wonder. A club looking to do well in

Europe would have fought tooth and nail to hold onto players like Moussa Dembele and Kieran Tierney; but money in the bank was more important. This policy of selling on talented players meant that Celtic, more and more, were reliant on domestic success. Some bloggers warned that Celtic were gradually weakening, but nobody paid any attention while the team was winning every trophy in Scotland.

Actually, whether the team was weakening or not was beside the point; it was the reliance on the domestic side of things that was Celtic's downfall. There might be glory in winning trebles and the like, but the fact is that there isn't a lot of money in Scottish football. The only real money-maker has always been the matches between Celtic and Rangers, and, more recently, Neo-Gers. This doesn't just guarantee a full stadium but brings in TV money from around the globe.

It was in Celtic's best financial interests to keep Neo-Gers going, especially since any European ambitions were stymied by the policy of selling players. And since staying in the black had become the be-all-and-end-all of Celtic's existence, maintaining the myth that the 'Old Firm' was alive and well suited the Celtic Board down to the ground. There was a problem, though. Neo-Gers were burning through money they didn't have. Such a situation couldn't last indefinitely and there was every chance that the new club might well go the same way as Rangers.

Financial considerations were not the only reasons the Celtic Board had to help keep Neo-Gers alive. There was the secret Five-Way Agreement. There has been constant speculation over what this agreement entails, but the truth is that nobody outside the signatories knows. Was there some sort of clause that forbade Celtic winning ten titles in a row? It's certainly not beyond the realms of possibility and, when you think about it, was more than likely to be the case.

The powers-that-be had been more than happy to go along with the Big Lie and had even let the new club pretend that it had already won 54 titles. As well as letting Neo-Gers claim the titles and trophies of Rangers, it stands to reason that some kind of provision was made to award the new club *future* trophies. After all, what was the point in a football club that only lived for the past glories of another, now defunct club? They were going to have to be allowed to win; and soon. But why this season in particular?

Nobody can have failed to notice that Celtic's past successes are usually ignored in the agnivores' desperate attempts to praise those of Rangers. For example, Rangers' appearance in a UEFA Cup final in 2008 is often remarked upon as if it were the high point of Scottish football in the last few decades. And yet, Celtic reached the same stage five years before. Equally, Celtic's Nine-in-a-Row under Jock Stein is forgotten; it's usually portrayed as Rangers' record, which Celtic only equalled in 2020. Were Celtic going to be allowed to surpass 'Rangers' record'?

Already in the summer of 2020, before the season even started, many Celtic supporters were talking about 'Operation Stop the Ten'. The subsequent shenanigans involving referees and Celtic players having to self-isolate showed that those supporters had been right in their predictions. However it was achieved, the Scottish football authorities went all-out to ensure that Celtic wouldn't win that tenth title in a row.

So, whether it was from their own financial self-interest, by dint of the Five-Way Agreement or the realisation that they were not going to be allowed to win the title this season, the Celtic Board knew that the game was a-bogey. At some point this message would have been passed on to Neil Lennon and his players. Of course, as many employees are, they would have been bound by confidentiality clauses in their contracts. They couldn't tell anybody what was going on, but it was obvious to any thinking observer that they weren't too happy about it.

When I was a teacher in Glasgow back in the 1990s, I spoke to many teachers that had been around since the 1980s. Among the stories I heard about that decade, one concerning school football came up time and again. Apparently, it was felt by some high-heid-yins that it was too much of a traumatic experience for children to be beaten comprehensively in a football match. To stop this happening, a rule was brought in that said if a team was leading by five clear goals, then the game immediately reverted to 0-0.

Of course, this resulted in school football matches being very strange affairs. Children soon learned, or were coached, to avoid scoring when they were four ahead. So, if a team were winning 4-0, they would thereafter just kick the ball about and defend in strength. A lot of children, mostly boys, were so pissed-off at 'not being allowed to win' that they packed football in altogether. Others enjoyed training but only took part in matches reluctantly, so disheartened that they made a lot of mistakes and didn't care too much when they did. Sound familiar?

Footballers are like big kids at times, in fact, all the time. During matches they throw themselves about, looking for free kicks and penalties, they look to get other players sent off and often react sulkily and petulantly when they're about to be substituted. Outside of game time, they're known for trying to get around club rules about diet, drinking etc. You can just imagine their reaction if they were told that they're not allowed to win the league and the best they can hope for is second place. Then again, you can hardly blame them; nobody would be entirely happy in that situation.

With the benefit of hindsight, one can see how up-and-down the Celtic players were in their matches. One week they'd be trying their hardest, the next they'd be behaving as if they were determined to lose or draw. Meanwhile, Neil Lennon sat in the dugout, arms folded, looking well pissed-off. He'd have loved to go down in Celtic history as the manager that won the Ten, but it wasn't to be. It must also have annoyed him immensely to read how much Celtic supporters were blaming him.[4]

Things came to a head in November, after Celtic were knocked out of the League Cup by Ross County. Crowds gathered outside Celtic Park, demanding that something be done and, more especially, demanding that Neil Lennon be sacked. The media, of course, exaggerated the story of what was happening, making it sound like a dangerous riot.[5] Even Sooperally commented, saying,

> I don't think I've seen anything like that in this country to tell you the truth, you sometimes see it when it's Turkey and Italy.

> It was absolutely shocking, an embarrassment, they really were, it goes without saying we can do without that.[6]

Sooper was obviously suffering from a selective memory as he seemed to have forgotten the behaviour of The People in Manchester in 2008. He'd also failed to remember how The People practically stormed Ibrox in January 2015 trying to oust Mike Ashley's board.[7] Naturally, the agnivores in the media followed suit, pretending that the demonstrations at Celtic Park were something unique in Scottish football.

At any rate, the Celtic support was adamant that Neil Lennon had to be replaced. And Lennon wasn't the only one getting it in the neck. Phil Mac Giolla Bhain has long railed against Peter Lawwell and his 'heated driveway,' and this season was no different. Neil Lennon didn't escape criticism, but Mac Giolla Bhain's main object of ire was Lawwell.[8] Others agreed wholeheartedly.

At the Celtic AGM in December, Peter Lawwell faced down his critics and confirmed that Neil Lennon would remain in place. He also maintained that Celtic would still win the title. In his defensive speech, there was one part that was quite telling.

> As always, our duty and responsibility is to do the right thing for Celtic.
> We've no other agenda, no other purpose or motive other than to make the right decisions for this great club.
> We haven't given up, it's going to be very difficult this year it's a big year for the league.
> We haven't given up and there are circumstances that have put us in this position, but we will go and do everything we can to get the league this year.[9]

What 'circumstances' did he mean? Was he talking about the SFA making sure that Celtic didn't have a chance? And as for doing the 'right thing for Celtic,' did he mean that the board had been put under pressure to let Neo-Gers win? Or, perhaps, he meant that letting Neo-Gers win the league to keep them alive was the 'right thing for Celtic' financially. Either way, it made a mockery of his assertion that Celtic could, and would, win the league.

The People and the agnivores had a field day, claiming either that Neo-Gers had improved immensely or that Celtic had regressed. Chowder Charlie Nicholas took the latter view, stating that the Celtic board had underestimated Neo-Ger's spending power and had been lazy in recruitment.[10] Another soup-taker, Andy Walker, slammed the Celtic board for its 'arrogance'[11] and branded it as lacking respect for, and being out of touch with, the supporters.[12]

This became a common theme on social media, and it was hard to disagree. The Celtic board was being so secretive it was as if they were running Neo-Gers! Celtic supporters were left nonplussed; how could a team that had so recently been winning everything deteriorate so rapidly? It was hardly surprising that they looked about for someone to blame. And there was no shortage of targets.

As well as Lennon and Lawwell, folk pointed to the lack of effort coming from the players. Rumours abounded that Edouard, and others, were keen to leave. If they did, they were hardly going about it the right way. Wanting to move to another club meant making that club interested in you. Who would want to buy somebody that went through a match as if they didn't care whether they won or not? Even if were allowed that Edouard was a great player ordinarily, nobody would want to buy a player that was obviously on the huffy side. That went for the rest of the team as well.

Now and again, Neil Lennon would have a public go at his players, saying that they were letting him down.[13] They were doing more than that. The Celtic board must have been terrified that the players were going to expose the whole shoddy reality about not being allowed to win the league this season. Pressure was no doubt brought to bear on Lennon to bring his players into line. They should at least *look* as if they were trying!

Nothing showed up how pissed-off the players were than the games against Neo-Gers, which, needless to say, they weren't allowed to win. The first game was at Celtic Park on October the 17th. We've already seen what happened at this match, with Celtic missing players due to Covid regulations and playing as if they'd never seen a football before. In the next match, at Ibrox in January, they put up more of a fight; that was, until Brother Boabby sent Nir Bitton off and reduced Celtic to ten men.

In the next match, at Celtic Park in March, by which time Neo-Gers had won the league, Celtic might easily have won if the referee, Willie Collum, hadn't made it plain that they weren't allowed to. Odsonne Edouard was cynically taken out in the Neo-Gers box. It was an obvious penalty but, instead of pointing to the spot, Collum showed Edouard a yellow card for 'diving'.[14] Edouard's wry smile and shake of the head showed that he understood fine well what was going on. In the last Glasgow derby of the season, the referee wasn't taking any chances and Callum McGregor was sent off in the 26th minute.[15]

By this time, Neil Lennon was no longer in charge. It was at the end of February, after a 1-0 defeat to Ross County, that Lennon was reported as having resigned.[16] Of course, there was speculation that he'd been sacked, but it seemed unlikely that the Celtic board would have deliberately got rid of somebody that was taking all the flack on their behalf. The truth was that Lennon was probably sick of the whole business, not least being blamed for everything that was going wrong.

Another hate figure among the Celtic support had already announced that he was going a month before Neil Lennon left. Peter Lawwell was staying until the end of the season, but his replacement had already been lined up; Dominic McKay, chief operating officer at Scottish Rugby.[17] No such replacement had been lined up for Neil Lennon, however, which suggests that the decision to leave was his own and came as a surprise to the board. The lack of a replacement manager, and the way the Celtic board seemed to drag their heels finding one, suggested something else.

It was glaringly obvious, as we have seen, that there was an agenda, anti-Celtic, pro-Neo-Gers or both, operating in the football authorities and even the Scottish Government. The question is, though, was the Celtic board itself part of that agenda? It certainly seemed so at times, and this was one of those times. Imagine a new manager arriving in March only to be told that he wasn't allowed to win the league. He'd be straight back out the door as fast as he could, contract or no contract, and he'd soon warn off any other prospective candidates. Everything would end up an even bigger mess than it was.

If we accept that the Celtic board was complicit in the team simply rolling over, then a lot of what we saw during the season makes sense. Whether the board was fully involved in helping to keep Neo-Gers afloat for financial reasons or just acquiesced to the plans of the football authorities is beside the point. Either way, they let the supporters down.

For weeks, there was constant speculation that Eddie Howe, manager of Bournemouth, would take over as manager of Celtic. This was eventually confirmed near the end of May, with Howe determined to bring his own backroom team with him.[18] It was hoped that he would be the one to carry out the rebuilding job at Celtic, if that, indeed, was what was needed. Essentially, though, all he needed was for he and his players to be allowed to win.

It was less than a week later that it was announced that the whole business with Howe had fallen through.[19] The Celtic board was at pains to point out that the fault didn't lie with it or Howe. Apparently, things broke down 'due to reasons outwith the control of both Howe and the club.'[20] What the hell did that mean? The man was a free agent, having left Bournemouth in August, so there was no other club involved to scupper either side's plans. Either the Celtic board had decided that Howe wasn't for them, or Howe had turned Celtic down.

There was rampant speculation about what happened. Some thought that maybe seeing the behaviour of The People put Howe off coming up here. Others opined that he wanted to stay in England and was looking to work for an EPL team. If that were the case, then he was to end up sadly disappointed.[21] Of course, it was possible that there was another reason entirely for his decision.

Neo-Gers winning the league was somewhat of an anomaly; a one-off that everyone involved worked hard to secure. It was something that we all knew, but we were all supposed to pretend otherwise, the way The People and the agnivores did. How would it look if Celtic were to win the 2021-2022 league when the story for the previous season was that Neo-Gers had improved? It was more than likely that all the stops would be pulled out to get Neo-Gers to the top once again. If Eddie Howe had sussed that one out, then he would hardly see the point in coming to Celtic, only to be blamed when things went wrong again.

It didn't take Celtic long to find somebody else, announcing Ange Postecoglou as manager in June.[22] Nobody had heard of him before, mainly because he'd always plied his trade in the Southern Hemisphere. He'd had a stint managing the Australian national team and was most recently in charge of Japanese team, Yokohama F. Marinos. In some ways, he's an unknown quantity but he seems to have been successful in his jobs so far. Apparently, he's in favour of attacking football and doesn't take any shit from the media. Time will tell. Then again, will he be *allowed* to do well?

Meanwhile, Neil Lennon was still hurting and lashed out at everyone except those that deserved it. He complained that his staff had been inherited, making things 'challenging'. He stopped short of blaming individuals, but the implication was that his hands were tied.[23] He also hit out at the Celtic support, saying,

> There was a new breed of supporters that I had nothing in common with and who belie the values of the club.[24]

He also called the supporters' 'obsession' with ten in a row 'unhealthy' and moaned about nothing being 'normal' in the midst of a pandemic. He complained too about the way Dermot Desmond and Peter Lawwell were treated.[25] What the hell did he expect? The supporters were confused and angry about the team seemingly going backwards and nobody was prepared to explain things or even apologise.

The supporters themselves were divided over Lenny's tantrum, some taking him to task while others agreed wholeheartedly.[26] As one supporter put it on Twitter,

> Maybe Lenny's right, fans are quick to blame everyone else but seldom look at themselves.[27]

Understandably, this comment caused outrage. How the hell could the supporters possibly be to blame? Unless Lenny was constantly on social media, he'd have no way of knowing how the supporters felt; they weren't allowed into the stadium, remember. It's not as if the team was constantly being booed and barracked by a fifty-thousand-strong crowd every two weeks. The reaction after the Ross County game was at the end of a long string of matches where the team underperformed. Lenny was attacking the wrong people.

Celtic supporters were, understandably, angry about their team's capitulation and, with Neil Lennon gone and Peter Lawwell on his way out the door, the board had nobody to hide behind anymore. More and more people were blaming them for the mess and wanted them out, or at least, to sell their shares to folk that cared, preferably the support itself.[28] Still, nobody seemed to mention that the board had acquiesced in the cheating that had gone on to let Neo-Gers win. The story persisted that Celtic had moved backwards while Neo-Gers had improved. On that score, the Celtic board had got off rather lightly.

They would also have got off lightly with another damning occurrence if Neo-Gers hadn't decided to spill the beans. It came after the destruction of George Square by The People in March. As everyone condemned the thuggery and violence, it was claimed that Neo-Gers hadn't done enough to disperse their supporters. Douglas Park took umbrage at this and wrote an open letter to Nicola Sturgeon, in which he blamed the police, who should have been prepared after the 'behaviour from the other half of the Old Firm outside Parkhead in December.'[29] Celtic replied to this in a tweet, which said, 'We're not half of anything…'[30]

This obviously annoyed the denizens of the Blue Room, and they were straight onto the press with a little revelation. It turned out that Celtic, along with Neo-Gers, had renewed the 'Old Firm' trademark at the Intellectual Property Office on the second of March.[31] The People had a field day, rejoicing in the fact that the Celtic board obviously subscribed to the Big Lie.[32]

James Forrest wrote to Celtic, asking for clarification. He was told,

> The trademark was registered to stop others profiting on the name and we renew it so that we may continue to hold that power; in short, we did it because as long as we hold the "rights" to it nobody can use it to market the term without our express okay.[33]

That 'nobody' included Neo-Gers, as James Forrest pointed out. Nobody was going to be able to use the term for financial gain. That seemed to clear things up. Or did it? James Forrest brought up another point, one that was hard to answer.

> My gripe is simply this; a definitive statement on this (that the Old Firm no longer existed) from the club would probably have an even greater neutralising effect than holding the trademark. If we completely washed our hands of it, in a public way, there is nothing to market on the back of.[34]

Although he brought this up, he didn't follow through, apparently content to accept Celtic's explanation that they were going down the legal route. His point, however, is a valid and important one. Why doesn't the Celtic board simply issue a statement denying the Big Lie and distancing itself from the new Ibrox club? The fact that it hasn't, but is content to creep about, keeping its signing up to the Old Firm tag a secret from the supporters, suggests something untoward. It seems to be the case that, although the right noises are made now and then to appease the supporters, the Celtic board is fully committed to the Big Lie and the continued existence of the club that calls itself Rangers.

The evidence is not what you'd call overwhelming, but it certainly seemed as if the Celtic board had been complicit in the great plan to hand the league title to Neo-Gers. But, had they done Celtic, or Scottish football in general, a favour in doing so? When it came to what The People called 'celebrating' there weren't many outside of the agnivores and The People themselves that thought so.

5
Party

On the evening of the 3rd of March, Livingston played host to Neo-Gers at the Tony Macaroni Arena, or Almondvale Stadium, as the media have started calling it again. It was a narrow 1-0 win for Neo-Gers, but the main story was all about Steven Gerrard being red-carded for arguing with the referee, Brother Boabby. Gerrard felt that El Guffalo should have had a penalty and the agnivores agreed with him.[1] Madden had booked El Guffalo for diving, a decision Gerrard disagreed with, so he shouted and swore at the referee at half-time. One can't help wondering if this scenario had all been set up; it allowed the agnivores to ignore a far more important story about the match.

There is a grass verge overlooking the Almondvale pitch and a large crowd of Neo-Gers supporters gathered there to watch the game. With no social distancing and not one mask between the lot of them, they celebrated the win with flares and fireworks. They were flagrantly breaking the law, but nobody seemed to be bothered, least of all Gerrard and his team, who went to salute them at the end of the match. The police didn't appear too bothered either and no arrests were made.[2] This hardly augured well considering the future plans of The People.

Those plans included carrying banners to Celtic Park to rub Celtic supporters' faces in it when their team secured the league title.[3] The problem with that, however, was that with Covid regulations in full force, there would be nobody around for them to lord it up over. They also planned a march to George Square, where they were going to celebrate their triumph in their own inimitable fashion.[4]

Why George Square? Their usual haunt was Glasgow Green, where they would congregate to get drunk after their annual July march. Glasgow Green, however, tends to be avoided by normal people when the Orange bigotfest is taking place. It would hardly suit their purpose with nobody around to flaunt their superiority in front of. George Square seemed a much better venue.

For years, Celtic supporters had been saying that Glasgow was green and white; now The People were determined to show them that it was not the case at all. George Square was the civic centre of Glasgow, with the City Chambers on its eastern side. What better place to declare that Glasgow was now red, white and blue? There was the added bonus that Queen Street Station was nearby. With any luck, there might be a few folk emerging to receive a good kicking.

There was a political aspect as well to the choice of George Square. When Labour were in charge of Glasgow Council, The People were convinced that they were all Celtic supporters and that helping their team was their overriding concern. Remember PZJ and all his crap about Celtic receiving preferential land deals? Now, there were even more hateful denizens of the City Chambers: the SNP. The whole event was being organised by the Union Bears, who, as their name implies, saw the SNP as the enemy. It was a good opportunity to rub the Nationalists' nose in it, especially with an election coming up.

We have already seen what happened outside, and inside, Ibrox on the 6th of March, when Neo-Gers beat St Mirren to only need one more point to secure the league title. Flares and smoke bombs were let off, while Gerrard and his players encouraged the blatant lawbreaking, hanging out the changing room window and passing drink around. One character got so excited that he pulled his knob out to have a ham shank![5] Glasgow, however, hadn't seen anything yet.

Celtic's miserable no-score draw against Dundee Utd the next day meant that, for the first time ever, Neo-Gers had won the league. The Celtic match had been a midday kick-off, which meant that The People knew their team were champions in the early afternoon. They congregated outside Ibrox Stadium to celebrate, letting off the usual fireworks and smoke bombs. Others gathered at George Square, obviously heeding the Union Bears' call.

The police were in attendance at Ibrox and moved The People on, away from the stadium. They didn't disperse the crowd, though. Instead, they gave them an escort along Paisley Road West and into the city centre so they could take part in the Union Bears' sash bash.[6] It was like an extra 12th of July for The People, banging drums and singing their songs of hatred, while the police walked beside them and did nothing.

The celebrations didn't just take place at George Square but all over Glasgow and beyond. To be fair, things didn't go on all night, most of The People going home about 9pm. That didn't stop it being annoying, though. Quite apart from the weans being frightened by the drums, singing and fireworks, folk were angry at following Covid regulations only for this lot to flout the law defiantly. As Muriel Gray put it,

> Finding listening to the endless noisy celebrations out the window tonight still going on all over Glasgow, where large groups of people are partying together with complete impunity a tad hard to bear. Makes you feel a bit of a mug for toughing it out and following rules.[7]

And it wasn't just by not adhering to the rules around Covid that The People were breaking the law. Drinking alcohol on the street is an offence as is urinating in public. The usual violent side of The People was in evidence as well, with the Celtic Store on Argyle Street having its windows smashed[8] and police officers being assaulted.[9] The surprising thing was that only twenty-eight arrests were made.[10] Then again, maybe that was not so surprising when you think about it.

A large clean-up operation had to be undertaken once The People had left, with huge piles of rubbish and broken bottles left behind in George Square.[11] There would probably have been a lot worse to clean up, including pish, shite and vomit. No doubt the press decided that nobody wanted to read about that kind of thing over their cornflakes!

As well as leaving the square in a mess, The People also indulged in a bit of vandalism. Benches were smashed and left unusable and probably beyond repair. That was bad enough, but the benches were memorials, paid for by families to remember their loved ones that had passed away.[12] Those families must have read the news in horror at what The People had wrought. The owner of the Louden Tavern started up a 'gofundme' page to raise money to pay for the damaged benches, saying that it had been 'accidental'.[13] There was a distinct whiff of entitlement about the affair, like the Bullingdon Club smashing up bars and restaurants and thinking they had a perfect right to because they paid for the damage.

Of course, there were recriminations as everyone looked to pass the blame onto someone else. The People indulged in their usual 'whatabootery',[14] while Neo-Gers tried to claim that they'd done everything they could to avoid the situation and blamed the Scottish Government.[15] The Chairman of the Police Federation laid the blame firmly at Neo-Gers' door,[16] but the police themselves didn't escape censure. Celtic supporters couldn't help but contrast how the police dealt with them as opposed to The People.[17] Whoever was to blame, though, the Scottish Government was clear: it shouldn't happen again.[18]

As a kind of coda to the whole sorry business, it was announced that some of The People that had attended the George Square Bash had tested positive for Covid.[19] Apparently, these individuals had disclosed this information when being interviewed (over the phone, presumably) about getting the test done. They must have been showing symptoms since free Covid tests weren't just handed out willy-nilly. It was recommended, however, that everyone that had been at George Square get tested.[20]

It wasn't mentioned if you needed to be displaying symptoms to have a test; probably not since they were being specific about those Neo-Gers supporters. It was doubtful though that any such tests would be booked. It's hard to imagine any of The People phoning up to say, 'Ah wiz wan-y the wans pishin' aw ower George Square an' smashin' up benches. Ah need a Covid test.' At any rate, none of The People seemed too concerned about the pandemic. It was somebody else's problem.

One display of triumphalism, however, wasn't anywhere near enough for The People. They'd been denied their usual bigotfests in Glasgow and Belfast during 2020 and it looked as if the same was going to happen in 2021. It was the Union Bears to the rescue once again, organising another meet-up at Ibrox with a march to George Square.[21] This was to take place on May 15th, the day Neo-Gers would be presented with the League Trophy. The two comments on James Forrest's blog echoed the sentiments of just about everyone; nobody would do anything to stop The People gathering, least of all the police.

Membership of the Freemasons is often seen as a *sine qua non* for advancement in all the UK's police forces. (Even Ted Hastings is a member - Mother of God!) In Scotland, the Masons are intimately entwined with the Orange Order and, consequently, Neo-Gers. It has long been suspected that the police in Scotland are overwhelmingly supporters of both Ibrox clubs. The softly-softly approach in March, along with the selfies with the Neo-Gers supporters tended to confirm those suspicions.[22]

In the week leading up to the 15th, it appears bars and restaurants around George Square were told to remove outdoor seating and to refrain from selling alcohol.[23] The People had been openly planning their 'celebration' at George Square, but nobody was going to do a thing to stop them. In fact, it looked as if they were going out of their way to accommodate them. Glasgow Council could easily have cordoned off George Square with the help of the police and Police Scotland had the powers to disperse crowds. They were not, however, going to use those powers. One person voiced the opinion of many as to the reason why:

> They never stopped the previous disgrace in the city centre and they won't stop this one the reason they say that they are powerless to stop it is lack of personal (sic) and that's because half of them have applied for time off so to join in the celebrations as they did the last time.[24]

Rather worryingly, The People were reminiscing about Manchester in 2008, saying what a great time they'd had.

Others were sorry that they'd been too young to attend and were going to make up for it at George Square. One even went way back, regretting that he hadn't been able to go to Barcelona in 1972![25] Just in case we'd all forgotten how The People had a 'great time', they thought they'd remind us. It certainly didn't augur well for Saturday the 15th.

The Council put scaffolding and fencing around the column, in the centre of George Square, which holds a statue of Walter Scott. It seemed a bit of a brainless move; even The People wouldn't be stupid enough to try to climb an eighty-foot column. Then again... Already, on the 13th, there were Neo-Gers flags hanging on the scaffolding.[26] The question was, though, why wasn't there protective fencing around the other, more accessible statues? Why just this one? One character had the answer.

> Its madness - and, I suspect, by design. If its still there it is inevitable that Rangers (sic) fans will get onto it. That immediately makes it dangerous, dangerous to the fans who climb on to it, no doubt in numbers way above its capacity, and to the fans below. The Police will have to act if that's what happens. They will have little real choice. And when they do? Who knows how that will end but we could all have a decent guess.
> In my view it is a trap laid by GCC. Nothing more, nothing less. To erect that scaffolding this week, of all weeks, is deliberate.[27]

This showed what kind of paranoid minds The People have. No doubt the Council sabotaged all the lampposts in Govan as well. One clown decided to climb one to put a Union Flag up. It appears the lamppost couldn't take his weight and collapsed, sending him crashing to the ground. He broke his hip, his ankle and his elbow and seriously injured his heel too.[28] He couldn't go to work afterwards, so somebody set up a 'gofundme' page, which, by the end of May, had raised £1,770.[29] He was lucky to have escaped with his life.

Another Hun on *Follow Follow* got his excuses in early too, also looking to blame Glasgow Council for any potential trouble.

> Accident waiting to happen btw. (He was referring to the scaffolding in George Square.)
> Never mind. We can't possibly open up a park to avoid any injuries. HSE ignored, I assume?[30]

This showed a complete lack of understanding of what the whole thing was about. What was the point of going to a park where there would be nobody around to rub their faces in it? Besides, there was the political aspect as well. The Union Bears had spent their time on the eve of the Scottish Parliament election putting up banners around Glasgow, urging people to vote tactically to get the SNP out.[31] They were hardly going to miss the opportunity to show Glasgow's SNP Council that they still had the upper hand. Meanwhile, planeloads, and probably ferry-loads, of Huns arrived in Glasgow from Northern Ireland.[32] They wouldn't take too kindly to being shut up in a park.

The Scottish Government and Scottish Police issued what the media called 'warnings' to The People not to gather at Ibrox or George Square. These 'warnings' were pretty toothless, however, and were essentially an appeal to The People, saying, 'Gonny no' dae that?' They should have saved their breath. Meanwhile, Neo-Gers themselves asked supporters to stick to the Covid guidelines.[33]

The big day arrived, and The People crowded around Ibrox Stadium to welcome the team. Steven Gerrard and his players made a mockery of the Neo-Gers appeal by greeting the mob, shaking hands etc. El Guffalo and Tavernier also went into the crowd, notably not wearing masks.[34] Gerrard should have been asking them all to go home, instead of encouraging them. Nobody came out of Ibrox to ask the crowd to leave either. The police *did* ask them to disperse but, as usual, there were no warnings, merely a plea for The People to take 'personal responsibility'.[35] Fat chance! The last thing any of The People ever do is take responsibility; everybody else is always to blame.

The pleas, of course, fell on deaf ears and, far from dispersing, The People climbed the gates and walls at Ibrox to see what was going on inside.[36]

Neo-Gers won the match 4-0, were presented with the League Trophy and it was party time for The People. As the good folk of Barcelona, Manchester and sundry other towns and cities can testify, a People's party is unlike any other party. Violence and destruction play a huge part and woe betide anyone that gets in their way. They certainly weren't about to let a little thing like a pandemic stop them! Unfortunately for the citizens of Glasgow, there was now an added dimension to The People's 'celebrations'.

Hands up if you remember *Ze List*. It was Chris Graham's online vow of vengeance, *The Enemies of Rangers*, which he started before his club died.[37] It was just the start of The People's blood-curdling oaths of what they were going to do once their team got 'back to where they belonged'. It was yet another consequence of the Big Lie, which I covered in the first book of this series, *Clash of the Agnivores*. Since everybody in the Scottish football authorities and in the media accepted the Big Lie without question, The People thought they had a perfect right to feel aggrieved. Since Neo-Gers was 'still Rangers' then there had been no need for the club to have been 'put down' to the bottom tier. They were all going to pay, and that glorious moment had arrived.

George Square took the brunt of things again, with the clean-up estimated at £58,000.[38] As well as all the rubbish and broken glass, the lighting around the Walter Scott column was smashed, there was graffiti everywhere and scaffolding and fencing were trashed. The benches suffered yet again, with most of them broken beyond repair, while hundreds of plants were destroyed. Even the traffic lights didn't escape damage. No doubt the Larkhall contingent took offence to the green ones!

The same mentality was responsible for the attacks on paramedics, who were spat on and called 'Fenian bastards' because they were wearing their standard green outfits.[39] It was fortunate that Glasgow was still in Tier 3, which meant that very few, if any, normal members of the public were around.

And that was another aspect of The People's behaviour that caused concern; their blatant flouting of the Covid regulations. They and their apologists, however, had a ready-made answer to these accusations.

On Thursday the 13th of May, a Home Office Immigration Enforcement van turned up at Pollokshields in Glasgow to arrest, and probably deport, two men. People from the neighbourhood quickly gathered in the street to block the van and stop it from leaving.[40] This incident, along with a pro-Palestinian rally in George Square on the 16th,[41] gave The People all the 'whatabootery' excuses they needed. Even on the 14th, before The People's disgusting behaviour occurred, unelected Tory MSP, Murdo Fraser was saying,

> I hope all Rangers fans will celebrate responsibly tomorrow, esp given the spike in Glasgow Covid cases. Sadly I fear such calls are undermined by some politicians actively encouraging street protests yesterday. Can't be one rule for some and another for others.[42]

Understandably, commentators tended not to mention the Covid breaches by The People. Instead, they concentrated on the wanton destruction, which went beyond the clean-up operation reported in the press. Statues of Queen Victoria and Prince Albert were damaged and would cost thousands to fix.[43] Ironically, these were the selfsame People that had flocked to George Square the previous summer to protect the statues from BLM activists.[44] Then there was the violence.

We have already seen how paramedics were attacked, but others suffered too. With nobody around to fight with, The People turned on each other. Folk were stamped on and beaten, with blood everywhere.[45] One has to ask, where were the police and what were they doing? They had their own troubles to contend with, with officers taking beatings that required hospital treatment.[46] Eventually, the police did what they should have done in the first place; they sent in the heavy mob, with riot gear.[47] The People responded by throwing missiles, including glass bottles and barriers, at the police.[48]

Interestingly, Police Scotland proved themselves far more proactive when it came to the upcoming Scottish Cup final between St Johnstone and Hibs. There was no pussyfooting about with calls to take personal responsibility this time. Instead, there were bloodcurdling threats of 'not hesitating to use powers' if any supporters stepped out of line.[49] Suspicions about The People being treated differently by the police were confirmed when one of their own was caught among the 'revellers'.[50] It would be interesting to put in a FOI request to find out how many other officers booked that particular day off!

While everyone condemned the disgusting scenes at George Square, Neo-Gers tried to distance themselves from them.

> Sadly, a small minority of people behaved inappropriately and in a manner not reflective of our support. Some of the scenes were unacceptable and have besmirched the good name of Rangers Football Club (sic). These so called "fans" should reflect upon the values and ethos of our club, and consider the damage this does to the reputation of the club.[51]

That sounded more like something from a parody account, but it was entirely serious. It showed either the lack of self-awareness of the club's board or its disingenuousness. That 'small minority' was entirely reflective of the club's support, as many could testify. That lie plus the insistence in calling the rioters 'so-called fans' showed that Neo-Gers were claiming that The People at George Square weren't 'real' Neo-Gers supporters. This claim was later to come back and bite them on the arse.

It was only the day after this statement that Neo-Gers tried to pass the blame for the George Square riot onto the Scottish Government. It was 'revealed' that Neo-Gers had asked the Scottish Government for permission for 10,000 season-ticket holders to watch the match and the trophy presentation *inside* Ibrox. The agnivores in the Daily Record said that the request had fallen on 'deaf ears'.[52] No prizes for guessing whose side *they* were on! The implication was that all the trouble could have been avoided but for the intransigence of the 'Raynjurz-Haturz' of the SNP.

This was entitlement to the max. Why the hell should the Scottish Government flout its own rules just to benefit The People? The main point of ridicule, however, was highlighted by many online. Neo-Gers had already claimed that the troublemakers in George Square weren't *real* supporters, so how could letting in season-ticket holders possibly have made any difference? Unless, of course, Neo-Gers were admitting what we all already knew to be true – those neds in George Square *were* real supporters. It was a move born of sheer desperation. It was as nothing, though, to the desperate claims of The People and their apologists.

One moron claimed that The People had been infiltrated by the Green Brigade and that four Celtic supporters had been arrested![53] Others leaped on Murdo Fraser's condemnation of the pro-Palestinian rally to claim that *they* were the ones that had damaged the statues. (Those tweets have mysteriously disappeared.) At any rate, The People simply couldn't accept that their own were responsible.[54] But it wasn't just the violence and destruction that was being condemned; a surprising new aspect had emerged.

Remember that bit in the Neo-Gers statement about the 'values and ethos' of the club? Although Neo-Gers and The People liked to pretend otherwise, everyone knew exactly what those values and that ethos were. Just like the old, dead club, at the heart of Neo-Gers was anti-Catholic bigotry and anti-Irish racism. Everyone is familiar with The People's disgusting songs, which were given an airing at George Square. No doubt the Northern Ireland contingent, the self-styled Ulster-Scots, delighted in telling those of us of Irish descent, without a hint of irony, to go home!

Most of us have heard these songs, like *The Billy Boys* and the *Famine Song* for years, so what was different this time? It wasn't the songs and chants themselves that were different; it was the reaction to them. For the first time ever, they were called out for what they were. The People might have been voicing their songs and chants for years, decades even, but they were always reported as being part of a two-way sectarianism between The

People and Celtic supporters. Now, it was as if politicians and the media had suddenly realised what The People's songs and chants were all about.

John Swinney, the Deputy First Minister, said it out straight on Radio Scotland, condemning the 'vile anti-catholic bigotry' of The People.[55] Nicola Sturgeon spoke too of 'vile anti Catholic prejudice.'[56] Humza Yousaf, the Justice Secretary, said pretty much the same and was supported by ex-BBC reporter, Jim Spence.[57] Even those masters of the anodyne and ambiguous statement, Nil by Mouth and Show Racism the Red Card, actually came straight out with it this time. In fact, they went further, condemning not only the anti-Catholic bigotry but the anti-Irish racism displayed by The People.[58] This was a first. Nobody in Scotland had ever acknowledged that such a thing existed before.

This theme was continued by others, such as Mike Dailly, Principal Solicitor and Solicitor Advocate at Govan Law Centre and Govanhill Law Centre. He struck the nail on the head when he said,

> In Glasgow and the West of Scotland, sectarianism has been used as a palatable euphemism for racism. What we've seen on our streets over the last weeks and months is racism against Catholics and people of Irish decent.[59]

Sectarianism implies that there are two sides, mutually antagonistic and equally as bad. This has always been the way things have been presented in Scotland, even though it's evidently not the case. And the idea that anti-Catholic and anti-Irish bigotry are simply West of Scotland problems is another myth. Anyone that has been to Musselburgh and other areas in East Lothian will know that it's not true. There are large pockets of Huns all over Scotland, aided, abetted and protected by a sympathetic Establishment. The Establishment wasn't going to take the truth being openly revealed like that lying down and ranks were quickly closed. The agnivores, as usual, were on hand to put the narrative right again.

BBC Scotland and the Daily Record dredged up Mark Walters and his bananas yet again to show that Celtic supporters were just as racist as The People.[60] Something they never mention is that such occurrences were common at football grounds in the 1980s; The People threw bananas in a similar manner at a Hibs player. They also ignore the fact that Walters joined in the anti-Catholic and anti-Irish singing of his fellow players.[61] What's that thing Jesus said about throwing stones?

There is another aspect of the harping back to this incident that shows plainly what the agenda is. Those bananas were thrown in January 1988, over thirty years ago. It was a full eighteen months *after* the banana incident that Rangers openly signed a Catholic in the shape of Maurice Johnson.[62] As many of The People love to point out, Rangers had signed Catholics before, but the truth was that it was done in secret and such players had to keep a low profile. The signing of Johnson effectively brought to an end the 'Protestants only' policy of Rangers, much to the chagrin of The People, many of whom burned their season tickets in protest.

The Scottish media like to present the signing of Johnson as having happened a long, long time ago. It's ancient history, something that belongs in the dim and distant past; after all, it happened over thirty years ago. On the other hand, 'Bananagate' occurred *only* thirty-odd years ago, as if it were just yesterday. It's disingenuous in the extreme and part-and-parcel of a disgusting agenda.

The truth is, there is little to no evidence of any bigotry emanating from the Celtic support, no matter how hard The People and their apologists try. And try they do; often desperately. For example, one of them put a video on YouTube, showing Celtic supporters singing when their team was playing against Linfield at Celtic Park.[63] He claimed that the songs they were singing, *The Broad Black Brimmer* and *The Merry Ploughboy*, were 'Sectarian and pro terrorist Ira'. Many would agree with him, but would they be right?

The rendition of *The Merry Ploughboy* could perhaps have done without the addition of 'Fuck the Queen' but that isn't what this character, and others, take issue with. Both songs are about the IRA of the early 20th Century and have nothing to do with its more modern counterparts. Even British history books speak of the 'Anglo-Irish War,' which means that the IRA of those days are considered to be *soldiers*, not terrorists. And what the hell this character can find sectarian in any of the lyrics is a mystery. If you listen to the video, you'll hear that the proper lyrics of *The Merry Ploughboy* are sung. There's nothing about bayonets slashing the Orange sash, so this clown doesn't even have that excuse.

The uploader of the video, in fact, is simply betraying his own anti-Irish racism. There's nothing offensive at all about the songs, unless, of course, you find anything to do with Ireland offensive. And that's the dilemma The People and their apologists find themselves in. Just because *they* hate the Irish it doesn't mean that everybody else does. I'm sure plenty of Nazis found *Hava Nagila*[64] offensive because it's a Jewish song and I doubt anyone would try to justify *that*!

Ultimately, The People depend on the belief, or, rather, the lie, that one side's as bad as the other. There are plenty of football rivalries in the world where teams' supporters positively hate each other. For The People, though, it goes way beyond that. Witness their lyrics to the Tiffany song *I Think We're Alone Now*[65] and the add-ons to Neil Diamond's *Sweet Caroline*.[66] It's not just Celtic supporters or even the Irish that they hate; it's all Roman Catholics. And, much though the likes of Nil by Mouth try to claim otherwise, there is no reciprocal hatred of Protestants exhibited by Celtic supporters.

The usual way of 'proving' that Celtic supporters are religious bigots as well is by use of the word *Hun*. The argument is that this is a slur against Protestants, much the same as The People's use of words like papes, taigs, tarriers, croppies etc. to demean Catholics, particularly Irish ones. The word *Huns*, however, has no religious connotations whatsoever; Nacho Novo might be a Roman Catholic but he's also a Hun. The word simply refers to anyone connected to Rangers and, by extension, Neo-Gers. (The vile support of Rangers 'tuped' over to the new club when the old one died.)

But, what about the legend 'KAH' (Kill All Huns) found daubed on walls in Northern Ireland and now appearing in

Scotland? Isn't that just as bad as 'KAT' (Kill All Taigs)? Well, no, actually. KAT is a slogan dreamed up by Loyalists and Orangemen in Northern Ireland, expressing a threat or a desire for all Catholics to die. KAH, on the other hand, is not a threat against Protestants, but against those anti-Catholic elements. And what football team do those anti-Catholics all support? Not that there's anything good about wishing anybody dead, but it's plain that KAH is not the widespread threat that KAT is, whether it's written by Northern Irish Nationalists or Celtic supporters.

Quite often the desperate attempts to show that Protestants suffer from bigotry just as much as Catholics can take an extremely ridiculous turn. One clown on Twitter claimed that the old Glasgow Corporation buses, which were green, white and orange, were an example of subtle anti-Protestant bigotry![67] The same individual, on the same thread, also put forward a blow-up doll wearing a Neo-Gers scarf, one of a few that were hung on nooses at Celtic Park a couple of years back, as another instance of anti-Protestant bigotry. One has to ask how the hell he makes that out. How does wearing a Neo-Gers scarf make you a Protestant? What happened to *Everyone Anyone*?

Others resort to downright lies. An Edinburgh Tory councillor, John McLellan, told, in the *Scotsman*, how he heard, while standing among Celtic supporters when their team was being beaten by Rangers, talk of 'stabbing Protestants'.[68] That he was *standing* in a football stadium shows how long ago it was, but that's beside the point. No matter how long ago it was, it was an unbelievable story. Also unbelievable were the excuses he made for The People.

> Lower education standards, limited job opportunities and Third World life expectancy in Glasgow are as much an influence as anything football clubs do or don't say.[69]

That's a strange thing for a Tory to come out with. Correlations between poverty and crime have long been proven, but the Tories have always denied that they exist. They have insisted that everyone is responsible for their own actions, whether they be gangsters, thieves, junkies or whatever. In fact, they've often claimed that there's no such thing as society. It seems, though, that The People are an exception. McLellan, inadvertently, explains why.

> There is a broader context, most obviously the association with unionism, and although there are SNP-supporting Rangers (sic) fans, the Queen's portrait in the home dressing room spells out the club's traditions.
> Rightly or wrongly, Rangers (sic) is about more than football and for 14 years the Scottish government has been run by a party which traduces the symbols and denigrates the country in which most supporters have been brought up to believe.[70]

In other words, they're all Tory voters, so excuses need to be made to keep them onside. McLellan's excuses fall short when you consider two things. Firstly, others have the same background and lack of educational opportunities as The People but don't behave the way they do. Secondly, The People come from all sectors of society with the only things uniting them being their hatred of Catholics and the Irish and their delusional sense of superiority and entitlement. Very few of the Huns you read about being arrested or up in court for various offences are jobless yobs; they tend to be in employment, often in well-paid jobs. The fact that off-duty police officers were involved in the scenes in George Square tells you that.

According to Graham Spiers, it had nothing to do with class, but a sense of being 'culturally left behind' that was to blame.[71] As many pointed out to him, nobody left them behind; they choose to be disconnected to the modern world. They, like many of their right-wing counterparts in England, want a return to the days when Britannia ruled the waves and the Irish and other Catholics, as well as black people, knew their place. Their traditional workplaces, where they were guaranteed a job by dint of being Protestants, have all disappeared, but they refuse to accept it. In their eyes, the world had no right to move forward; it should have stayed where it was.

Such hatred and fear, coupled with a sense of superiority only has one outcome: paranoia. The People have developed a whole belief system, based on this paranoia, in which the Irish, their co-religionists and woolly-minded liberals and socialists have conspired to destroy Protestants' religion and way of life. Normal Protestants don't feel this way at all; only The People, who believe that they are the only true Protestants left in Scotland and, of course, Northern Ireland. One character online compared the 'plight' of The People to that of the Tutsi in Rwanda in the 1990s. Among his insane ramblings, he managed to sum up the opinions of most, if not all, of The People.

> Equally malicious, throughout Scotland, the history of our people is being erased. The Reformation, the most important and consequential event in Scottish history is ignored, as is the plight of the Covenantors. The Church of Scotland, or what's left of it, manned by middle class, chicken hearted apologists, scared and embarrassed by their own shadow (think John Swinney, Ross Greer), has betrayed its sacred charge and commission and in doing so abandoned its people.
> Rangers (sic) remain the strongest, in fact only Protestant and Unionist institution of note and power in Scotland. That's why our enemies are so desperate to destroy us, we are the last and only line of defence.[72]

The immediate reaction to this individual's polemic is one of hilarity, but, when you think about it, it's quite frightening that there are people among us that believe this nonsense. Some of the replies to the post are worth reading too in order to get a sense of the burning anger and violent purposes of The People. It's even more frightening when you realise that there are folk in positions of authority, like the police, the judiciary and the Scottish and UK Parliaments, that subscribe to this rubbish as well. Meanwhile, those that don't subscribe endlessly pander to them or even manipulate them for their own ends.

In the thread we looked at above, with the guy that compared The People to the Tutsis in Rwanda (with little regard for the truth, I might add), both he and the people replying to him see Unionism, in the shape of the Tory Party, as their only hope.[73] The Tories, for their part, encourage this belief and are among the loudest and most forceful in making excuses for The People.[74] In many ways, The People have become the stormtroopers for the Tories in Scotland. If they really want to take lessons in history, they'd be better off reading about the *Night of the Long Knives*!

Also involved in making excuses for The People are the Scottish media. Even when they're condemning the vile behaviour of The People, they either bring Celtic into it or shrug their shoulders in helplessness. Look at what Hugh Keevins says about the bigotry that surrounded Rangers and now surrounds Neo-Gers.

> And, to be fair, that questionable culture was subsequently addressed by the signing of Catholic players and the appointment of a Catholic manager in Paul Le Guen.[75]

The implication there is that the boards at Ibrox have done all they can to stamp out anti-Catholic and anti-Irish bigotry. But have they? If that's so, then why do they keep having orange tops in their third strip? And what's the deal with the wee anti-Irish dig in their song *Follow Follow*? In fact, there are plenty of instances of ex-players of the old team attending 'sash bashes,' where they join in, and often lead, the singing of songs of bigotry. The current board, meanwhile, indulge in whatabootery whenever the filthy singing of The People is criticised. Either that or they ban the reporter completely, which is what the current refusal of the BBC to go to Ibrox is about. Then, we have the current players.

Remember that drinking session that was held in a function suite at Ibrox after the final game of the season? There was more to it than breaking Covid protocols. The players, and others, were all singing along to *Sweet Caroline* and decided to sing The People's add-on, 'Fuck the Pope.'[76] Well, some of them did. It's clear from the video that a number of them were singing, 'Doo-doo-doo.' It was reported in the press that the police were investigating the incident.[77]

Neo-Gers, of course, denied everything, talking about 'trial by social media' and claiming that the video had been 'doctored'.[78] Actually, 'doctoring' a video like this is a lot harder than you might think. The easiest way, in fact, the only way, unless you're an expert, would be to use an audio track taken from another source. It would take a while to align the video with the audio, which would have to be done in minute detail to make sure the gestures in the video are consistent with the sounds. You'd also need a decent editing software, like Sony Vegas, which will set you back around five hundred quid!

The majority of your time, however, would be taken up with finding suitable footage from which to get the audio. This would be a process of trial and error as you attempted to secure footage in which nobody suddenly shouts out, 'Happy birthday, Senga!' or something similar. In fact, this could take you days and would require the kind of patience that most folk simply don't have. It seems a hell of a lot of bother to go to just to make up stories about some football players being bigoted.

The above would need to be done on a PC and it's extremely doubtful that it would be ready for upload on the very night the incident took place, as happened on this occasion. In fact, it's well nigh impossible. Interestingly, if you look at the video again, you'll see someone being stopped from videoing the 'fun' by, presumably, a security guy. What reason would there be to do this unless it were to keep something hidden? And, as many folk pointed out, the easiest refutation would be obtained by Neo-Gers simply uploading the 'undoctored' video. This, however, never happened.

Before anyone accuses me of hypocrisy, I'm aware that I claimed that a video purporting to display racist abuse of El Guffalo had been 'doctored'.[79] Doing such a thing would be a relatively simple process, especially compared with the Neo-Gers video. It would mean making a short, secondary audio track with just someone shouting the offending term. Both tracks could then be merged with the video, and nobody would be any the wiser, especially since there's no video of the alleged perpetrator, just background noise.

Anyway, Police Scotland, in its wisdom, decided that Neo-Gers and their players had no case to answer.

> In relation to a video circulating on social media showing Rangers players allegedly using sectarian language on Saturday 15 May, extensive enquiries have been carried out and no criminality has been established.[80]

And that was all they had to say on the matter. No reasons were given for their conclusion, and nothing was said about the video being inauthentic. Neo-Gers, however, thought they'd been vindicated and released one of their many statements, threatening dire consequences for all.

> RANGERS (sic) welcomes the outcome of the Police Scotland investigation into a video involving some of our players and staff.
> Whilst we were confident that no criminality took place, we recognised that we had a duty to assist Police. Furthermore, given some of the attempts to spread false narratives, we had to protect the reputation of individuals involved.
> This is a stark reminder to those in senior positions within society who should be cognisant of their influence, responsibility and the consequences of their actions on others.
> We can confirm that we have initiated legal proceedings against certain individuals for comments made this week.[81]

One of those individuals was the then Justice Secretary, Humza Yousaf, who had said on Twitter:

> I have also been made aware of this clip, *if* (and I stress *if*) this clip is genuine then any player or staff member

found to be guilty of anti-Catholic hatred should be shown the door by the Club.
It is right Police Scot investigate & determine the facts around it.[82] (My italics.)

Thousands of Huns signed an online petition to call for Yousaf's resignation,[83] while others called for him to apologise.[84] It was difficult to see what he had to apologise for. He couldn't have been more explicit that his expected action was conditional on the video being proven to be accurate. One would expect that Neo-Gers, with their much-vaunted inclusivity, would have been all for sacking the guilty players in the unlikely event that Police Scotland decided that the incident was worth pursuing.

The Tories tried to make political capital out of Yousaf's statement,[85] while some of The People set up a crowdfunding site to
help Neo-Gers sue those that had 'sullied the reputation of our Club's board, management, players and staff.'[86] The People, however, are known for having short arms and deep pockets and are no doubt aware of how badly their club has fared in other court cases. Consequently, the fund has scarcely raised enough to pay for a couple of hours of a solicitor's time.[87] In fact, some of the pledges are obviously from piss-taking Celtic supporters and are unlikely ever to be honoured.

After this, the furore over anti-Irish and anti-Catholic bigotry not only died down but disappeared altogether. By the end of the month, the Herald felt confident enough to publish a piece claiming that deep-seated anti-Catholic and anti-Irish prejudice was no longer a widespread problem in Scotland.[88] And a group of women shouting anti-Catholic abuse and then pishing all over the steps of a Catholic church in Glasgow was a story that was ignored by the mainstream media.[89]

The final nail in the coffin came from Police Scotland, who, near the end of June, reported that the video of the Neo-Gers players singing 'Fuck the Pope' *had* been doctored.[90] As I explained above, this is a remarkably difficult thing to do and seems unlikely, especially considering the video was uploaded almost immediately. I believe big, Hollywood producers are now looking for the individual responsible for the video. He's got a great career ahead of him in sound syncing and editing.

Meanwhile, the Daily Record reported on abuse aimed at the actor Martin Compston, a well-known Celtic supporter. The abuse was no longer called 'anti-Catholic' or 'anti-Irish', but simply 'sectarian'.[91] Aye, it's jist banter, intit?

6
I Am A Poseur

Folk that subscribe to the theory that Neo-Gers improved in season 2020-21 point to their long run in Europe as proof. The agnivores, of course, praised the team to the hilt, making out as if they were the new Barcelona or some such. The truth, however, was a lot more prosaic. In some ways it resembled the old Rangers' run in the UEFA Cup in 2008, when they benefited from easy opponents and sheer luck. It helps, though, when you're able to make your own luck.

The qualifying games for the group stages of the Europa League were pretty straightforward. Lincoln Red Imps and Willem II are hardly what one would call big names in Europe, while Galatasaray didn't have their troubles to seek during 2020. Covid hit the club in May[1] and three players had to isolate in November.[2] In September, one of their key players missed the game against Neo-Gers after displaying flu-like symptoms. His Covid test was negative, but the Turkish team wasn't taking any chances.[3]

This became a theme during Neo-Gers' Europa run. Standard Liège were missing three players, who had tested positive, when they faced Neo-Gers in October.[4] Benfica had the same problem when they played Neo-Gers in November, as well as having players injured.[5] It was a problem that hit many, if not all, football clubs in Europe; in fact, it was a worldwide problem. Top teams were the worst hit as their players returned from international matches testing positive. Only one team seemed to be lucky enough to avoid any players testing positive. Then again, was it really luck that was involved?

What the actual procedure was for taking samples, I've no idea, but I would imagine that the players did their own swabs and sealed them in the appropriate plastic cannisters. It made sense for the samples not to be taken by UEFA officials or medical personnel; there was the chance that this could spread infection. This, of course, would provide the opportunity for a bit of cheating.

As with practically all Covid testing, a private company was in charge of doing the tests for UEFA.[6] We already saw, in an earlier chapter, how Channel 4's *Dispatches* programme and the BBC's *Panorama* had shown poor procedures, and maybe even corruption, in UK Covid-testing labs. Now, far be it from me to cast aspersions on Synlab, the company carrying out the tests for UEFA, but there's one thing that's paramount in private companies – profit. Making sure the shareholders are paid their dividend is the bottom line.

Companies, even companies involved in health care, want to maximise profits and do so by charging clients as much as they can get away with. They also do it by trying to keep employees' wages as low as possible. Expert scientists aren't going to work for peanuts, so they're hardly going to be employed doing the tests; their role would be supervisory. The actual, day-to-day tests would be done by folk with a lot less qualifications. After all, they just needed to dip the swab sticks into some kind of chemical solution and record what sort of reaction happened.

The upshot is that a player could stick his swab stick up a dog's arse and nobody would be any the wiser. We're not talking about DNA analysis here; all the testers were doing was looking for a specific chemical reaction or the lack of one. Such a system would obviously be open to abuse.

Of course, I might be unfairly maligning a group of conscientious workers, all trained to the highest standards in all things medical. Perhaps the swabs were taken by individuals trained for the job and not by the players themselves or anyone connected with the team. Besides, Neo-Gers wouldn't cheat, would they? At any rate, Neo-Gers managed to make it unscathed through to the knock-out round.

Neo-Gers also rode their luck somewhat when it came to the referees. They were as thuggish as they usually were but seemed to get away with it. It wasn't the way it was with Scottish referees, and they certainly didn't get away with everything, but they engaged in plenty of what the agnivores like to call 'meaty tackles'. It was inevitable that they would eventually come up against a team just as thuggish as they were, and that team came in the shape of Antwerp.

The first leg, in Belgium, was more like a battle than a football match. Seven yellow cards were shown, one of them a second, which resulted in a sending-off for the Antwerp player. Three penalties were awarded, two for Neo-Gers and one for Antwerp. Neo-Gers won the game 4-3.[7] In the return leg, at Ibrox, four yellow cards were dished out and Neo-Gers won 5-2, with two late penalties helping out.[8] Neo-Gers were through to the last sixteen.

It was also inevitable that Neo-Gers would come up against a team that was better than they were, and one not plagued by injuries and positive test results. The first leg against Slavia Prague in the Czech Republic wasn't a harbinger of anything special, resulting in a 1-1 draw.[9] It was in the second leg, at Ibrox, that Slavia's superiority showed through, with Neo-Gers not being able to score at all. They could only resort to sheer thuggery as Slavia put two goals past them to win the match and progress to the quarter-finals.[10]

As usual, excuses were made for Neo-Gers, whom the agnivores still gushed over as a vastly improved team of world-beaters. The BBC Scotland website said,

> Having been rocked in the opening 45 minutes of the first leg - which came just four days after their Scottish Premiership title win – Rangers (sic) improved in the second half in Prague and carried that in to the opening exchanges at Ibrox.[11]

Oh, aye, that home game against St Mirren must have taken a lot out of them, eh? Slavia's win, though, wasn't deemed the most important aspect of the game. The aftermath of the game went on and on for ages in the Scottish press. Even the violence of certain Neo-Gers players took second place in level of importance. And violent they most certainly were.

Neo-Gers kicked, tripped and pushed their way through the match and Slavia were lucky not to get a couple of penalties.[12] Balogun ended up with a second yellow for scything the legs from under a Slavia player. He also had a kick at the player while he was on the ground.[13] Then there was Kemar Roofe.

Roofe was sent on in place of Scott Arfield in the 55th minute. He'd only been on the pitch for a few minutes when he received a long pass to send him in on goal. The ball bounced in front of him and, as the Slavia goalkeeper came toward the ball, Roofe went in high with his studs showing. He clattered right into the Slavia goalie, sending him sprawling with blood spraying from his head.[14] It was a disgusting spectacle and Roofe was lucky not to face arrest at the end of the match.

Although everyone agreed that Roofe deserved to be sent off, (everyone except, apparently, Alex Rae[15]) excuses galore were made for him; he had his eye on the ball, it was too late to pull out etc. One has to ask, though, if Roofe only has one eye and no peripheral vision. Even if he was concentrating on the ball, he must have been aware of the Slavia goalkeeper coming towards him. It's notable that he didn't run to head or chest the ball down to his feet, as most players would have done. Obviously, he didn't want to get hurt himself in a collision with the goalie. It was a cowardly move, calculated to ensure that only his opponent would get hurt. And, in the context of how Neo-Gers behaved in this particular match, it's hard to argue that it wasn't deliberate.

When the match was over, the Slavia players and staff were left out on the pitch and weren't allowed into the changing rooms for about half an hour. In fact, they weren't even allowed into the tunnel. You might remember that March 2021 was a pretty cold month, and you can see that the players were doing their best to keep warm.[16] They could have ended up with pneumonia or something similar.

It looked as if the Czech media weren't allowed inside either; the reason for that soon became clear. Steven Gerrard announced to the assembled media that one of his players, Glen Kamara, claimed to have been racially abused by a Slavia player, Ondřej Kúdela.[17] Slavia Prague's president denied the allegation later that evening.

If you watch the video of the Slavia players and staff left outside in the cold, you don't need to be able to understand

Czech to realise how angry they all were. And you can hear somebody say what sounds like *polizei*.[18] In fact, Slavia *did* call the police as they claimed that Kúdela was physical assaulted in the tunnel at the end of the match.[19]

In the comments section of a video analysing Roofe's red-card incident, somebody had this to say,

> Dangerous tackle from Roofe, deserved a red card.
> No complaints there.
> Nice to see the Czech fans attaching this totally unrelated incident to their racist player to deflect.
> As cowardly as your player.[20]

Actually, that was the accusation Slavia Prague levelled at Neo-Gers, claiming that it was all a cover-up to deflect from the thuggery of the Neo-Gers players. They also mentioned the assaults on their goalkeeper and Kúdela. In one part of the statement, it said,

> The pending investigations conducted by the officials of UEFA and the local police have made no findings so far. However, our player Ondrej Kudela has already been the subject of a public 'conviction' without any evidence whatsoever; he is a victim of prejudice and a presumption of guilt.[21]

Now that sounded familiar. Compare it with the complaints from Neo-Gers we saw earlier about 'trial by social media' over the bigoted singing of their players.[22] In fact, 'trial by media' was a common complaint from The People.[23] They honestly seemed to think that the SFA Compliance Officer watched *Sportscene*'s analysis every Sunday just to look for an excuse to retroactively punish Neo-Gers.[24] It appeared, though, that they were perfectly happy for everybody else to face 'trial by media'.

And tried in the media Kúdela and Slavia Prague most certainly were. Whenever Slavia made counter-allegations against Neo-Gers, the accusations were called 'pathetic', 'astonishing' and 'unfounded'.[25] The Czech Republic national team's claims of being against racism, meanwhile, were branded 'hypocritical'.[26] The Scottish media had already made their minds up and Kúdela was guilty as hell.

Forgotten in all the furore was the Slavia goalkeeper, who had to have stitches and suffered a fractured skull.[27] Kemar Roofe was given a four-match ban for the assault, which many considered rather lenient. Neo-Gers had the gall to appeal the decision, but UEFA threw it out and upheld the ban.[28] The People, meanwhile, continued to claim that Roofe was innocent and denied also the accusation that Kúdela had been beaten up in the tunnel. One of them had an interesting take on this point.

> Rangers (sic) have denied this and Police Scotland said they have had no knowledge of it. Making claims like this, with no evidence, can be extremely damaging.[29]

Er…wasn't that what Neo-Gers and the Scottish media were doing with Kúdela? Michael Stewart pointed this out on the BBC's *Sportsound*, urging caution when it was one man's word against another. His fellow pundit, Richard Foster, argued the opposite, saying,

> And I know we don't know, but if we go down the road of 'it's an allegation, we don't know' then we're never going to know.[30]

That sounded like Foster was saying that the word 'allegation' should be dropped and that everybody should just assume that Kamara was telling the truth. He went on,

> And the punishment should be individual for the player, he should get a year's ban, the club should be thrown out of this year's competition and banned for next year.[31]

I wonder what team he thought should take Slavia's place in the competition; probably the one that the Czech team had just knocked out. It's worth pointing out that Foster is an ex-Neo-

Gers player and is married to the singer Amy Macdonald, who is a high-profile Hun. Not exactly a disinterested observer, then.

When he was speaking, Michael Stewart mentioned another incident, earlier in the season, when Neo-Gers players accused Michael Gardyne of making a homophobic slur against El Guffalo. The SFA charged him with breaking the rule on 'threatening, abusive, indecent or insulting words or behaviour'. The charge ended up being dropped, however, with no explanation given.[32] Some folk speculated that perhaps it had been discovered that the Neo-Gers players had possibly misheard what Gardyne said.

Everybody was sure that there was no mistake this time and Michael Stewart was attacked from all sides, especially by The People.[33] Club 1872, meanwhile, demanded that Stewart be sacked by the BBC.[34] Nobody was prepared to even admit the possibility that Kamara had made an error. So, a Finn heard a Czech whispering something in English and there was no mistaking what he heard? It would hardly stand up in a court of law.

Then came a new twist. It turned out that Bongani Zungu had heard what was said as well.[35] So now we had a South African thrown into this multinational mix. Somebody with too much time on his hands analysed what happened on YouTube, arguing that Zungu only reacted when he heard Kamara complaining to the referee that he'd been racially abused.[36] The uploader also implied that Kúdela had not had time to say what Kamara was accusing him of saying. It was all quite inconclusive, but it showed that there were questions that needed answered. In fact, there were a couple of inconsistencies in the story.

Steven Gerrard claimed that Kamara told him that he'd been racially abused once the match was over. Gerrard also said, however, that he tried to call Kamara over to the side of the pitch to see if he wanted to leave the field.[37] Walking off the pitch in disgust has become the standard form of protest toward racism in football. That would suggest Gerrard was aware that Kamara was racially abused. So, which was it?

And the waters were muddied even more when Kamara implied that Kúdela had whispered into his ear.[38] Earlier, Gerrard had explicitly stated that the Czech player had *shouted*.[39] Then there was Connor Goldson, who, although he admitted he hadn't heard what Kúdela said, claimed he had 'never been so angry on a football pitch.'[40] Actually, he'd appeared just as angry about what Michael Gardyne was alleged to have said,[41] and we all know how that turned out!

Kúdela, meanwhile, wasn't doing himself any favours with his account of what he'd said to Kamara. Kamara claimed that Kúdela said, 'You're a fucking monkey, you know you are.'[42] The Czech player, however, insisted that he'd said, 'You fucking guy.'[43] It hardly seemed likely, unless, of course, he'd mistranslated some idiomatic Czech expression. The truth probably lies elsewhere.

Over the last few years, some folk online have taken to calling Huns 'monkeys'. It's obviously not meant as a racial slur, but as a comment on the low intelligence evident among The People. Imagine, though, if somebody were to use the word in relation to a black Neo-Gers player. They'd be condemned as a racist and all the arguing in the world that the word hadn't been meant that way wouldn't convince anyone. The agnivores would have a field day and The People would believe all their Christmases had come at once. It's a remarkably stupid thing to do, using words that can be easily misconstrued and it's obviously better to avoid them altogether.

This could possibly be what happened in Kúdela's case. He's used a word in the heat of the moment that he's subsequently realised could be understood as being racist. Rather than trying to explain himself to a sceptical public, he's desperately backtracked and painted himself into a corner. Even if he said something that wasn't racist or couldn't be considered such, he might well have said something that could easily be *misheard* as racist. Regretting saying whatever it was he said, he came up with a rather unbelievable account on the spur of the moment. If he were to now change his story and explain what he actually said, he'd be branded a liar as well as a racist.

Also not helpful to Kúdela's case was all the racist abuse sent over the internet to Kamara and other black Neo-Gers players. Kamara and his lawyer bore the brunt of it, especially after Kúdela received a ten-match ban from UEFA.[44] It was all very well sticking up for your team's player, but the actions of the Slavia support made it look as if Kúdela *had* uttered something racist and the Slavia supporters were right behind him.[45]

A Czech vlogger had a different story to tell.[46] He pointed out that Kúdela spoke very little English and it was possible that Kamara had misheard him. This is actually a valid point. How many of us that have studied French, Spanish or German at school know what the word for 'monkey' is in one of those languages? I did French, Spanish, Latin and Ancient Greek at school and college and French is the only language I can say 'monkey' in. So, how the hell would Kúdela, a man knowing very little English, know what 'monkey' meant and its meaning in the context he was supposedly using it?

The vlogger also claimed that the Czech Republic was not a racist place at all, while Prague was a multi-racial city with very little, or no, conflicts between the different races. In fact, he claimed that the way everyone had assumed that Kúdela was guilty showed racism against Eastern Europeans. Some of the posters on his vlog pointed out that the Czechs were Central Europeans, not Eastern, but they missed the point. What the vlogger meant was former *Eastern Bloc* countries. And he wasn't far wrong. Poles, Czechs, Croatians, Serbians etc. have all suffered from prejudice in Britain, especially after Brexit. In fact, Neo-Gers themselves currently had a problem in that respect.

Erald Krasniqi, who came to Scotland as an asylum seeker when he was a child, had worked at Ibrox for thirteen years, working with both Rangers and Neo-Gers. The Daily Record described him as a 'kitman', but he was more than that. He also worked as a youth coach and was on a salary of £45k a year. He was sacked for allegedly stealing some Castore gear and was attending an industrial tribunal to argue that he had been unfairly dismissed. He apparently had a long catalogue of accusations of the racial abuse he'd received at Ibrox to recount.[47] Strangely, I haven't been able to find any more details about this industrial tribunal and what happened at it. Maybe others that are more knowledgeable about such things might have better luck.

The People, of course, questioned the timing of this revelation, claiming, as usual, that the Scottish media had it in for them. (Do they actually read the same papers as everybody else?) One character said,

> Basically, been caught stealing and now playing the race card.[48]

Now, *there* was a case of pots and kettles if ever there was one! Slavia Prague had the same to say about the allegation of racism coming from Neo-Gers. Their side of the story was that the allegation was made to cover up Neo-Gers' thuggery and the near killing of the Slavia goalkeeper. It wasn't the first time Neo-Gers had played the race card. Ever since El Guffalo had arrived in Scotland, they'd been saying that referees and the football authorities pick on him because he's black. El Guffalo's agent was at it again in March, claiming that his client was treated differently from other players.[49] It was hardly surprising that folk were a bit sceptical about Kamara's claims.

The People couldn't help but express some racism of their own, proving the point made by that Czech vlogger.

> Theiving (sic) cvnt. Why oh why do w@nkers like that get a job that thousands of paying Rangers (sic) fans would die for?
> 45K for an asylum seeker to sort out some strips...I don't fuckin think so.[50]

> Ive (sic) worked with plenty of Eastern Europeans and they are amongst the most racsist (sic) people on the planet. I was genuinely shocked how much hatred they have for black people. Its either ingrained in their society or I just happened to work with the wrong ones.[51]

Oh, dear! Of course, The People would point to the racist abuse being directed at the black Neo-Gers' players as proof of how racist the Czechs were. That piece of inductive reasoning, however, would go against one of Neo-Gers' main excuses for the behaviour of their own supporters. How often have we heard that it's just a 'minority' that sing the bigoted and racist ditties and delight in destroying property? If they couldn't accept that other teams have a minority of troublemakers, then how could anyone believe their constant claims that only a minority of The People were responsible for the bigotry and violence associated with their support?

Another aspect of the whole business was, of course, totally ignored by the Scottish media. It concerned Steven Gerrard. It was nearly ten years ago that Liverpool hosted Manchester United at Anfield. The main talking point of the match was when Luis Suarez of Liverpool racially abused United's Patrice Evra. It was similar to the Kamara/Kúdela incident in that it was one man's word against another's. And, just as happened with Kúdela, Suarez was found guilty and received an eight-match ban from the English FA.[52] What was different was the reaction of Gerrard to the affair.

In concert with everyone else at Liverpool, including manager Kenny Dalglish, Gerrard supported Suarez. They all refused to accept that Suarez was guilty and wore tee-shirts declaring their support for their teammate.[53] Although Evra has since received apologies from those connected with Liverpool at the time, Gerrard has never apologised.[54] It made his stand against racism and his stated belief that Kamara was telling the truth sound like nothing more than hypocrisy. It appeared that Gerrard was only prepared to believe that racist abuse occurs when it happens to one of his own players.

But that was all in the past, wasn't it? What was the point in dredging up stories that were already history? Nobody does that and certainly not the Scottish media. Unless, of course, the story happens to concern Mark Walters and bananas!

Anyway, the Scottish media continued their hypocritical condemnations with numerous articles about Romanian player, Nicolae Stanciu, refusing to take the knee when his country's national team played England in a friendly. He explained that, as a Slavia Prague player, he was protesting at his club colleague being banned from playing 'without any proof'.[55] Notably, the same media appeared to be fully behind Neo-Gers when *they* refused to take the knee before their next game at Celtic Park.[56] It was in protest at UEFA seemingly not doing anything substantial about racism. The Celtic players, rather shamefully, remained standing as well, while other Scottish teams joined in this 'protest' in sympathy with Neo-Gers.[57]

This was getting needlessly confusing. So, on the one hand we had players standing in protest at their friend and colleague being found guilty of racism, while others stood as a symbol of their fight against racism. Connor Goldson explained his reasoning for choosing to stand:

> I'll be honest, taking a knee - token gesture from the higher authorities to make it look like they are doing something to help. But they are not because when these things happen there is no consequence.[58]

That's not what he'd been saying the previous June, when he was online, arguing with The People, who weren't happy with their team taking the knee. The Neo-Gers supporters claimed that they weren't racist but didn't like the socialist politics behind the Black Lives Matter movement.[59] Goldson had this to say, alongside of a picture of him taking the knee:

> This isn't about politics it's about equality!!! We all need educating, myself included![60]

The Neo-Gers Managing Director, Stewart Robertson, told those supporters criticising the players taking the knee that they wouldn't be welcome at Ibrox, while Jermain Defoe spoke of players taking the knee as being 'powerful messages'.[61] The People, however, weren't interested in such messages, powerful or otherwise. The truth was that the stuff about BLM being socialists and the like was nothing but a smokescreen for their racism.

When Connor Goldson complained about the abuse he and others were receiving online back in July 2000, he said it was 'disgusting,'[62] which strongly implied that it was nothing to do with politics and everything to do with racism. He also said that it was 'not surprising,'[63] which meant that it wasn't the first time black Neo-Gers players had been racially abused by their own supporters.

In fact, The People have a long history of racism and part of Ibrox Stadium had to be closed because of this in August 2019.[64] The football authorities and the Scottish media have long pandered to The People, insisting that their anti-Irish racism is sectarianism. And, needless to say, Neo-Gers always pander to their bigoted support as well. They might make the right noises about being against racism and bigotry, but they know as well as everyone else that the bigots in their support are in the majority, not the minority they always claim. If they were to take any real action against these bigots, then it's doubtful they'd have any supporters left.

As if to show how racist they are, The People introduced us to a new addition to their repertoire of delightful little ditties during their 'celebrations' in May. There was one particular video doing the rounds showing a young blonde woman, with teeth that belonged on a Grand National winner, singing said new song.[65] (A word of warning if you intend watching the video. You'll jump back at one point, certain that she's about to take a chunk out of your face!) Her teeth were also unnaturally white, prompting some folk to liken her to Methadone Mick from *Still Game*. The woman ended up being arrested for her very public racism.[66]

The song in question was to the tune of *Ye Cannae Shove Yer Granny Aff a Bus* (or, if you prefer, *She'll Be Comin' Round the Mountain*). The lyrics, as you might expect from The People, were pretty simple: *Oh, Ah'd rather be a P**i than a Tim*. Another video, though, might have helped the woman with the equine gnashers to claim that she wasn't being racist at all.

Step forward Abdul Rafiq, who was also in a video singing this charming song, although he substitutes the word 'Tim' with 'Taig'.[67] He also sings, *Ah'd rather wear a turban than a cross*, which seems anti-Christian rather than specifically anti-Catholic. Still, so long as it entertained the ones taking the video, which it obviously did, as you can hear from all the laughter. He is also told, 'Go!' at the start of the video, which implies that he was encouraged to sing the song for his audience, who probably taught him it.

The truth is that the guy is a few channels short of the full SKY package and the ones he hangs around with rip the pish out of him without him realising. He's like the eponymous character in the Woody Allen film *Zelig*, who desperately wants to fit in. Rafiq pops up everywhere you find fascists and racists, at EDL rallies and the like.[68] Of course, they all pretend to be his pals and use him to make out that they're not racists or bigots. The People use him for the same reasons. And Rafiq is obviously loaded, with rich parents or some such, considering the vast amounts he's had to pay in fines!

Back to The People, and they'd shown, both with their online complaints and their public racism, that Neo-Gers players taking the knee for BLM wasn't for them. With the possibility of supporters being allowed back into football grounds in the new season, albeit on a limited basis, Neo-Gers had to be proactive. The whole story of 'standing against racism' was just a rationalisation. The truth was that they didn't want the world seeing their supporters booing their own players and showing everybody how racist they really are. In fact, it wouldn't be at all surprising to discover that the whole Kamara/Kúdela saga was invented expressly for this purpose.

It wasn't just Neo-Gers that were worried about racist supporters. When England faced Croatia in their first game of the Euros, they were booed by their own fans when they took the knee. Not all the England supporters did this; many of them applauded, trying to drown out the boos. The ones booing were obviously Brexity types, who were opposed to BLM because of their racism. It had happened at the start of England's last two friendly games as well.[69] The England team decided to ignore the racists and defiantly keep taking the knee.[70]

The Scotland squad, meanwhile, decided to do the opposite. They were going to stand at the beginning of each of their games, whether others took the knee or not. Steve Clarke explained that the decision about whether to take the knee or not was left to the players and, a short while back, they'd decided they were going to stand.

> At that time, the Scottish players were hugely frustrated with the seeming inefficacy of the gesture of taking the knee, after Rangers (sic) midfielder Glen Kamara was subjected to racist abuse from Slavia Prague's Ondrej Kudela.[71]

Actually, it seemed more than likely that the decision was made by some high-heid-yins in the SFA. That bit about Glen Kamara gives the game away. For years, most of The People have refused to support the Scottish national team. A Hun called Jeff Holmes, who makes his living writing books about Rangers and Neo-Gers (probably with lots of pictures for the illiterate majority among The People),[72] explained why in the Daily Record.[73]

There was a load of pish about English players at Ibrox and Paul Gascoigne scoring against Scotland (whose goalie in that game was Andy Goram), which provided neither reason nor excuse for abandoning Scotland. Then he got around to the 'grievances':

> In 1994, the SFA had done something similar to Rangers striker Duncan Ferguson when they whacked him with an unprecedented 12-game ban for a 'phantom' headbutt on Raith Rovers player John McStay. It was a disgraceful punishment and Big Dunc refused to play for Scotland after that.[74]

What? Did he mean the Duncan Ferguson that served a three-month prison sentence for the deliberate assault on John McStay? And remember, he had two convictions before that, one for headbutting a policeman and another for beating up a man with crutches. Apparently, he was on probation at the time he headbutted John McStay.[75] Ferguson was a thug and a cowardly bully, who deserved everything he got. It just shows how the minds of The People work, though, when they consider Ferguson hard-done-by.

Holmes continued, bringing us to the real nitty-gritty:

> For me, though, the dam burst in 2012. The SFA put the boot into Rangers when the club was on its knees; when we needed help from our governing body, and that help was nowhere to be seen.
> Our club was a mess. We're the first to admit it, but the way we were treated was appalling.[76]

The People, of course, agreed wholeheartedly, putting the case a lot more forcefully than Holmes did.

> Steve Clarke is a Rangers-hating wank who fills his teams with other Rangers-hating wanks.[77]

> Three reasons?
> Just one - Celtic's infiltration of Scottish football in the attempt to kill out (sic) club.[78]

This paranoid crap had put the SFA in a quandary ever since those halcyon days of 2012. Rangers had always been the establishment team and, when it died, the football authorities were happy to go along with the Big Lie. It suited their purposes to pretend that Rangers still existed, but that, of course, caused problems. If the team at Ibrox was still Rangers, with a continuous history, then there should have been no need for the club to start over in the bottom tier. This is The People's argument, that their team was 'demoted' without cause. The SFA and the SPFL haven't gone as far as apologising to Neo-Gers and The People, but you get the impression that they regret what happened all the same.

Our football authorities have been desperate to get The People back onside, as witnessed by everything that was done to help Neo-Gers win the league. That, however, wasn't enough for The People, who believe that their team won the league by its own efforts. The SFA has therefore done its level best to make the Scotland team attractive again to The People. They've gone out of their way to choose Huns for the team, even though they've proven to be useless, like Oli McBurnie.

The truth is that Neo-Gers don't have too many Scottish players to be chosen for the national team, but the SFA has tried its best. That's why Jon McLaughlin and Nathan Patterson were chosen for the squad, along with ex-Neo-Gers player Billy Gilmour.[79]

That, however, wasn't anywhere near enough to satisfy The People, who believe the whole Neo-Gers team should be taking the field for Scotland, whether they're Scottish or not! So, what better way to suck up to them than to pretend that all the players are right behind Neo-Gers' decision to stand instead of taking the knee? It would mean that Neo-Gers could go on pretending that the decision has nothing to do with their racist supporters.

In their first game against the Czech Republic, the Scotland players *did* stand instead of taking the knee. The Czechs, of course, were still refusing to take the knee in sympathy with Kúdela, who would have been playing if it were not for his ten-match ban. It was quite a repulsive sight, twenty-two white players (Che Adams was on the bench) all standing as if they couldn't give a toss about racism. It didn't matter what excuses or rationalisations they came up with; it wasn't a good look. But then, surely, like the England team, they would stick to their guns and wouldn't care less about how it looked. Actually, they cared very much how things looked.

The next match was against England at Wembley, and it was going to look rather odd with the English players all taking the knee and the Scottish players standing. The England team had several black players, and it might well look as if the Scotland team was just a gang of racists. Speaking of racists, how would the Brexiteers among the England support react to the Scottish players standing? It didn't bear thinking about. Therefore, it was decided that the Scotland players would take the knee along with their English counterparts.

Scotland's next game, and, as it turned out, their last, was at Hampden against Croatia. As the players all stood, there was the embarrassing spectacle of the Argentinian referee taking the knee, then, realising he was the only one on the pitch doing it, standing up again.[80] Why the Croatia team was standing was anybody's guess. A spokesman said they weren't taking the knee simply because they didn't have to.[81] Well, that explained nothing! As for why Scotland was standing instead of taking the knee, the Scotland captain, Andy Robertson, explained.

> Our position was - and remains - that the focus must be on meaningful change to fight discrimination in football and wider society.
> In Scotland, the football family has stood against racism all season. It was our collective view that the national team would do the same.
> Our stance is that everyone, players, fans, teams, clubs, federations, governing bodies and governments must do more. Meaningful action is needed if meaningful change is to occur.[82]

Now, that didn't sound rehearsed at all, did it? It also sounded totally disingenuous. That bit about teams in Scotland standing against racism 'all season' was a blatant lie. All teams took the knee until Neo-Gers' contretemps with Slavia Prague. That's when things changed. Neo-Gers decided to stand, and, to their shame, other Scottish teams followed suit. The fact that everybody had to lie about why they weren't taking the knee showed how embarrassed they were about kowtowing to The People.

It begged the question, of course, of what players in Scottish teams would do next season. Many people are of the opinion that taking the knee has become a meaningless gesture, but that's utter nonsense. If it were meaningless, then why would it rile all the racists so much? Neo-Gers, of course, will remain standing and we all know the reason why. Other clubs following suit shows that they're standing (pun intended) with Neo-Gers and therefore siding with racists. And the anti-Irish racism and anti-Catholic bigotry at Neo-Gers will continue unabated, with our media happy to go along with the myth that it's a sectarian, two-way street.

Which brings us back to Glen Kamara. In his statement after the Kúdela incident, he had this to say,

> There is no place for racism or any form of bigotry in football. Since Summer many of us have taken the knee

> in solidarity with those who have lost their lives to racial violence.
> If UEFA genuinely wants to 'show racism the red card', then it's time to stop the tokenism and take a zero-tolerance approach.
> As a player, I do not expect myself, nor any other to have to tolerate racial hatred on or off the pitch in 2021.[83]

That's pretty unequivocal. He's against all forms of bigotry in football, or so he says. Interestingly, Kamara took part in the Scottish Cup quarter-final against St Johnstone, which, you'll remember, St Johnstone won on penalties. The reason why it went to penalties was the late goal scored by Zander Clark, the giant St Johnstone goalkeeper. Okay, it touched Christopher Kane's leg, but it was Clark's header that sent it on its way into the net.[84] As you might imagine, the Neo-Gers players and staff were none too happy and somebody among them let their feelings get the better of them.

There is some debate over what, exactly, was shouted and over who was being shouted at, but two words stand out clearly: 'Dirty Fenian!' Even after several listens, it's difficult to make out what he's telling the 'dirty Fenian' such-and-such to do, or what noun is being qualified with the word 'Fenian', but that doesn't matter. The racist slur is there for all to hear.[85]

Of course, there was no mention of this anywhere in the media, only online, where some people claimed not to hear the offensive word at all. James Forrest, the blogger, e-mailed several people, MPs, Show Racism The Red Card etc. but only one character, a member of the Scottish Government as far as I can make out, bothered to reply. He said, among other things, that,

> I am certainly willing to condemn all forms of racism whether linked to football or anywhere else. However, what I will not do is take sides between Rangers (sic) and Celtic. Both have a hard-line support who go beyond the bounds of reasonableness but which the two clubs do little to

curb. They claim these supporters give the stadia atmosphere and I assume they also benefit from the money coming into the clubs from these fans.[86]

In other words, 'Shut it, Timmy, your lot's just as bad!' Forrest was taken aback and pretty angry (understandably) at this reply, especially, as he pointed out, there were no supporters in the stadium. It had to be someone actually employed by Neo-Gers. (It was hardly going to be somebody connected with St Johnstone.) As such, it would be relatively easy to find out who it was as the tirade was delivered in a strong, Scottish accent. Nobody, however, was even remotely interested.

The People use different methods to try to deny that the word 'Fenian' is racist or even sectarian. One is that Celtic supporters often call themselves 'Fenians,' which is a pretty specious argument and disingenuous. It's like those racists that claim it's okay to use the 'N' word because they've heard black people call each other it in movies. Another is that the word refers to a Nineteenth-Century Irish nationalist group. Again, though, that's a nonsense argument.

Yet another is that if the word is directed at someone that is not a Catholic, has no connection with Ireland or Celtic, then it's meaningless. This is all tied in with The People's belief that outlawing such words is part of some huge, Catholic conspiracy. It's a stupid attempt at justification but, then again, we're talking about The People here and brain cells are in short supply among that mob. How can a word be considered racist or sectarian when the person being shouted at is manifestly *not* a Fenian by any definition of the term.

Most people believe the abuse was shouted at Zander Clark, which makes sense since it was his presence in the box that resulted in the goal. As far as I can discover, Zander Clark has no connection to Ireland, is not a Catholic and doesn't support Celtic. In fact, his brother is a Neo-Gers supporter,[87] and it is believed that the rest of the family are as well.[88] In that case, the word 'Fenian' is meaningless, at least, it is in The People's eyes. The only ones offended are outsiders watching the clip and *looking* to be offended.

There are a couple of things wrong with that assessment, not least of which is if the term is meaningless, then why use it? There is also the little matter of Neo-Gers and The People getting all riled up about an alleged homophobic term being aimed at El Guffalo.[89] Was Morelos coming out of the closet or was everybody at Neo-Gers outing him? If not, then the term was meaningless, wasn't it?

Anyway, we heard nothing at all about this episode of anti-Irish racism in the media and Glen Kamara, strangely, didn't think it worth mentioning. Perhaps we're being a tad unfair on Kamara, though. His first language isn't English, so maybe he misheard what was said!

7
Obsessed With You

Do you remember in 2007 all the kids getting a day off school and coming home with commemorative mugs? Some companies even gave their workers a holiday, while some places were festooned with flags and bunting and there were street parties all over England. There were programmes on the telly practically the whole day, looking back over the Queen's reign. Actually, none of this happened at all, but it should have done. After all, it was the Queen's Emerald Jubilee;[1] fifty-five years on the throne. And 55 is a very special number, isn't it? Well, it seems to be to The People at any rate. (Though, you'd better not mention emeralds to them.)

Ever since 2016, when Neo-Gers made it into the Premiership, The People had boasted every season about how they were going to win and how Celtic supporters were going to be in tears, if not suicidal. '55 is going to end them,' was a favourite saying on their forums and in comments on newspaper articles. Quite why Celtic supporters would get so upset about a number nobody explained. The People, though, were extremely excited about the prospect.

> This is the younger Generations CWC1972 or 9IAR, for me just immense pride that we made it back to our rightful place on top of the throne. What a journey, never to be forgotten never to be repeated and every word from every Struth quote will ring true. There will be tears of that I am sure.[2]

> Bit p*ssed here but when I think of 55 I get emotional. The thought of where we were, what

> others tried to do to us and what it means......
> everything!!! My kids don't know a successful rangers
> (sic) team, that needs sorted.[3]

So, really, The People were just desperate for their team to win the league, so they could show *theym* and show everybody. All their paranoia and hatred were tied up in not just winning, but in beating *theym*. Their whole sense of superiority and entitlement hinged on this.

> This year will mark the 2nd decade long drought ive experienced as a Rangers (sic) fan. If the celebrations are anything like they were in after the 1st one it will be a day to remember. I've seen some great Rangers teams in my life, I've seen us win many trophies, but 55 will likely top them all for the simple fact that we came close to extinction. We were robbed, striped (sic) bare, and left in the gutter for dead. Little by little we clawed our way back and now stand on the threshold of being the best once more. Whether or not we win it this year when it does come it will mean we are back on top, where we truly belong.[4]

Although this last character, along with others of his ilk, appeared to be prepared to be patient and wait for 'when it does come,' the truth was the exact opposite. The People knew as well as the rest of us did that this season was the last-chance saloon for Neo-Gers. If they didn't do it this season, they never would. In fact, they'd be fortunate to even exist anymore if they didn't win the league. That, however, still doesn't explain the obsession with the number 55.

You'll have noticed among the quotes from Follow Follow above, and among other comments on the forum, that mention of the younger generation pops up. This was a great concern of The People. There were teenagers among them that probably thought that green and white ribbons were an integral part of the League Trophy. Neo-Gers decided to disabuse the younger generation of this notion and let them know to whom the trophy *really* belonged.

'Rangers (sic) fans across Scotland & Northern Ireland now have the chance to see the trophy in all its glory!' was the announcement.[5] Yes, Neo-Gers were taking the League Trophy on tour, giving The People the opportunity to see it up close and personal. It was £35 for a ticket that admitted two. A couple of time slots were set aside for families, with the same priced tickets admitting four from the same household, so the weans could see that the trophy was 'coming home'. As an added bonus, the ticket price included having a professional photo taken alongside the trophy.[6]

Throughout July, the League Trophy would be traipsing around Scotland, appearing at different towns and cities from 9am until 5pm each day. Tickets were valid for a half-hour session, but it was quite probable that multiple tickets would be sold for each session.[7] That meant that it would be in the door, stand in a queue, get your picture taken and then back out the door. The price seemed a bit steep for what you were getting and several of The People moaned about it online.

> after the last year when many of us have spend (sic) 100s if not 1000s supporting the club, would it have killed them to give this free to season ticket holders. A full season plus about 5 games from the previous season with no refund and they couldnt even let us get a picture for free[8]

> There's a thread laughing at the mentally challengeds (Celtic supporters) because their club thanked them for buying a season ticket and refunded them a gift voucher for £50.
> We get offered a chance to see the trophy for £25. (This was the price for *MyGers* members.)
> Beginning to think our loyalty is getting taken for granted.[9]

Despite the complaints, the events sold out quickly and, by the end of June, there were very few tickets left.[10] Strangely, there was no mention of any dates in Northern Ireland, even though it had been explicitly stated in the Twitter post that the trophy would be appearing there. Then again, July is a busy time for The People in the six counties. They have pallets to steal, huge ziggurats to build, Irish flags and pictures of Catholics to collect, tyres to burn, marches to go on, copious amounts of alcohol to consume, popes to fuck and fights against each other to have. Perhaps Neo-Gers decided that it would be better to go over at a later date.

Of course, the trophy would be festooned with red, white and blue ribbons but, although they'd be pleased to see that, The People would demand something more. Either attached to the cup or in plain sight on whatever piece of furniture it rested on, the number 55 had damned well better feature prominently. There had already been complaints galore about pieces of memorabilia *not* displaying the magic number.

It was back in March, when Neo-Gers clinched their league win, that an announcement was made regarding a commemorative chocolate bar.

> Rangers (sic) and Cadbury have come together to create a limited edition Dairy Milk Champions Chocolate Bar.
> Just 10,000 bars will be made available and include a commemorative letter from Steven Gerrard.[11]

The price of the chocolate bar was £7.10, which seemed a bit steep but nowhere near as expensive as some of the other commemorative products that were available.[12] For the majority of The People, a bar of chocolate it was going to be. Opinion was split over whether the bar of chocolate was a rip-off or good value, but many of The People decided that they would buy one or more.[13] Once they'd bought them, though, they were none too happy. Well, they never *are* happy, but they were even less happy than usual.

There was nothing particularly special about the chocolate bar itself. It was just a 95g or 100g bar, which costs around £1, with a cardboard sleeve on it. As

105

described in the Daily Record, the cardboard sleeve (not the wrapper) depicted various things to do with Neo-Gers.

> The wrapping on the bar includes a collage of images and signs for the likes of Ibrox's Bill Struth Stand, "The Twelfth Man" (A tribute to Scotland's referees?), "Nine in a Row" and their Romanian attacker Ianis Hagi.[14]

And therein lay the problem. As one of The People complained,

> £8 for this @RangersFC (sic) you are having a laugh here surely. A cardboard packaging with a £1.29 chocolate bar inside. No mention of 55 on it... hardly the champions range that you've been promoting. Fuming.[15]

When asked if he'd received the advertised letter from Steven Gerrard, he replied,

> I did mate. That's the only thing that mentions 55 and clearly the only reason they inserted it. It's not a limited edition chocolate bar, it's a limited edition chocolate sleeve.[16]

You'll notice that his main gripe was that the chocolate bar and its cardboard sleeve didn't mention '55'. On a side note, some characters weren't bothered about what it said on the chocolate bar or the bit of card surrounding it; they put it straight up on e-Bay to see if there were any suckers willing to pay double for this 'piece of history'. One chancer was even asking fifty quid for it![17] It was still there, unsold, in July; of course, it might have stood a better chance if he/she had asked for £55!

You no doubt already know why they were obsessed with the number 55; it was to, in The People's minds, prove that the continuity myth, the Big Lie, was true. It was difficult to know who they were trying to convince. None of us normal people were going to be taken in by the Big Lie no matter what happened or what anyone said. After all, it had been shoved down our throats for about eight years and we still didn't believe it. So, who was all this '55' guff aimed at? The answer to that was simple; themselves.

No matter how thick and gullible The People are, the truth is that even *they* know that the team they follow is no longer Rangers. All the rubbish about engine-room subsidiaries, holding companies, clubs not being companies etc. etc. and even the desperate Pacific Shelf nonsense simply go to show that The People and their like clutch at any straw available to deny the truth, that Rangers died. '55' is just another crutch.

There was, of course, another reason why the number 55 was so important to The People and to Neo-Gers; it expressed an enormous sense of relief. For a long time, it looked as if Celtic might reach that magic figure before Neo-Gers had the chance to pretend to do so. It was something the agnivores tried desperately to ignore and even Celtic supporters rarely discussed.

As we all know, mainly because The People and the agnivores never stopped telling us, Rangers' title win in 2011 was their 54th. Whether anybody believed that this made them the 'World's Most Successful Club' or not, it was important to The People's sense of superiority. Celtic had only won 42 titles and were obviously way behind Rangers in the 'World's Most Successful Club' league. Things, however, had changed a lot since then.

Amid all the excitement of treble trebles and a second Nine-in-a Row, it went unnoticed that, in 2020, Celtic reached the milestone of 51 titles. Just four more and they would surpass Rangers' beloved record. It must have sent a shiver up the spine of every Hun, agnivore and denizen of the Blue Room. Even if one subscribed to the Huns' contention that Celtic's title win in 2020 was only 'three-quarters of a title,' 54¾ is still more than 54! And, using The People's own criteria, Celtic would become the 'World's Most Successful Club'!

The collective feeling of utter relief throughout Scotland in March 2021 was almost tangible. Not only had Neo-Gers stopped Celtic reaching ten in a row, they had also stopped

Celtic's relentless march toward beating Rangers' record. So, '55' wasn't just a symptom of the Big Lie, it was a huge GIRUY to Celtic for failing, as yet, to beat, or even equal, Rangers' record.

So, were Rangers really the world's most successful club? The answer is totally dependent upon who you ask. Ask any Hun or agnivore and you already know what answer you'll get. Others, though, use different criteria. The Daily Mirror, for example, used trophy count to determine that Egyptian club, Al Ahly, was the most successful football club in the world as of August 2020. Al Ahly had a grand total of 118 trophies, while Rangers were in second place with 115.[18] Celtic were fifth with 106. Since Rangers were dead, however, they wouldn't be adding any more to that trophy haul.

As one character pointed out in the comments section, Al Ahly actually had more than 118 trophies; 140, to be precise.[19] Wikipedia agreed with this assessment, outlining all the trophies the Egyptian club had won to date.[20] Even if one were to accept the Big Lie, Al Ahly would still be well out in front for many a year.

Another list, this time by the Daily Star, had Rangers and Celtic as the numbers 1 and 2 clubs, with Al Ahly in third place. According to this, Al Ahly only had 107 trophies to their name.[21] This was because they discounted the old Cairo Cup competitions that Al Ahly used to take part in. It was hardly their fault that the country used to be divided into regional leagues. It would certainly keep The People happy, though.

Strangely missing from these lists was the Northern Ireland team, Linfield FC. Even when the team *was* mentioned on a list, said list got Linfield's number of league titles totally wrong. For example, the *Sportbible* website has 'Rangers' as having the most league titles in Europe, 55, including Neo-Gers' 2020-2021 title, with Linfield second on 53.[22] The *Soccerladuma* website, in 2019, had the same positions, with Rangers on 54 and Linfield on 53 when listing the most league titles in the world.[23] Those figures were correct at the time. Linfield, however, won the title in both 2019-2020 and 2020-2021, meaning they had really won 55 titles. *Sportbible* had somehow conveniently overlooked this fact to keep 'Rangers' in top place.

So, really, the top club in the world in terms of trophies won was Al Ahly, while the top in terms of league titles was Linfield. Not that Linfield would be crowing about the fact. If you look at the club's website there is nothing at all about being the 'World's Most Successful Club' or the like.[24] In fact, you need to delve into the 'Club History' section under the 'Club Information' menu to even find a mention of them having won 55 titles at all.[25] There is, of course, a reason for this.

As Linfield FC well knows, although its fan base lives in the locality, Linfield is actually the *second* team of the majority of the supporters. Their first team is Neo-Gers and they're all staunch adherents of the Big Lie. If Linfield were to claim that they were equal with Neo-Gers or, God forbid, started going on about dead teams and the like, they'd soon find that they'd have hardly any, or even no, supporters left at all.

For their part, The People didn't want to share what they perceived as *their* record with anybody else, even Linfield. They felt they didn't need to share since they didn't recognise Linfield's 2019-2020 title win. The Irish League had been abandoned that season and, just as in Scotland, the title had been decided on a points-per-game average. Since The People didn't recognise Celtic's title win for that season, it stood to reason that they wouldn't recognise Linfield's either. One character summed up the feelings of The People,

> Any title awarded is tainted. We're still the most successful and it was done properly on the pitch.[26]

How many times have we heard *that* one? If any titles were tainted, they were those ones that Rangers got through cheating. And as for what The People called their 55th title, that was won in the back rooms of Masonic lodges, rather than on the pitch!

There was yet another significance to the number 55, a rather sinister one. It was a symbol that 'Rangers' were 'back' at the summit of Scottish football, as Neo-Gers vice chairman, John Bennett confirmed.

> We are back where we belong at the top of Scottish football, but there is an awful lot more still to be done to make sure we stay there.[27]

He wasn't just concerned with keeping Neo-Gers at the top of the league, though. He also said, 'I know what was done to my club,' and spoke of how Neo-Gers had 'scores to settle both on and off the pitch.'[28] For almost nine years, The People had threatened revenge on all their perceived enemies. It looked as if the club itself was doing the same.

Mention was made in Chapter 5 of *Ze List*, Chris Graham's infamous rogues' gallery of the 'Enemies of Rangers'. Rangers subsequently died, but the so-called enemies were 'tuped over' to Charles Green's new club. Since then, the list has grown somewhat, with many new names added. There were, and are, however, some characters and organisations that have been consistently on the list throughout the nine years since *Ze List* first made its appearance.

Chief among these enemies are the football authorities, the SFA and the SPFL, which The People and Neo-Gers believe are under the thumb of Celtic. Quite how they make that out is anybody's guess, but there it is. This means, though, that they have to ignore the facts that are staring them right in the face.

First of all, they wouldn't be able to claim that they'd won 55 titles if it weren't for the football authorities accepting the Big Lie. The People and their club, however, aren't exactly renowned for their gratitude. In their eyes there are no lies involved. The club they now follow *is* still Rangers and Scotland's football authorities are simply facing 'facts'. There's therefore no need for any gratitude. In fact, the evil bastards did their best to kill Rangers and 'demoted' them to the lowest division in the league. It's been a case of the football authorities cutting their own throat since The People wouldn't be able to have these opinions if the SFA and SPFL didn't accept the continuation myth.

The SFA have also bent over backwards to accommodate Neo-Gers. Their match officials have consistently helped the Ibrox club with penalties given to Neo-Gers and denied to the opposition. They've also turned a blind eye to the thuggish behaviour of El Guffalo and others. Remember, Neo-Gers went through the whole 2020-2021 league campaign without a single red card. And, in February 2021, the SFA appointed one of The People as Compliance Officer.[29] And not a thing has been done about the breaches of Covid Regulations at Ibrox, including Nathan Patterson and his cronies turning up at someone's house for a party. The Huns, though, still insist that Scottish football is run for the benefit of Celtic.

Then there's the media in Scotland, which Neo-Gers and The People constantly complain have got it in for them. One BBC reporter happened to mention the bigoted singing at Ibrox a couple of years ago and the whole BBC has been banned from the place ever since. According to The People, this kind of criticism is commonplace when the truth is completely otherwise. Any mention of the bigotry of The People always has to bring Celtic into it, with the old myth that 'one side's as bad as the other.'

The media help in other ways too. The papers always give free advertising to any event connected with Neo-Gers under the guise of reports. Any article telling everyone about Ibrox events or 'sash bashes' and the like always ends with information about how you can get tickets. The printed media in Scotland have also tried their damnedest to get El Guffalo sold for the past few years. One can perhaps forgive The People for believing otherwise. The simple fact is that most of them can't read!

Among the individuals, top of the list as far as Neo-Gers and The People are concerned, is Mike Ashley. This guy is enough to put shivers up and down the spines of everyone connected to Neo-Gers. The story is that he's gone, but there's always the fear that he's still there, in the shadows, like the bogeyman. And it's the corpulent figure of Mike Ashley that betrays the problem at the heart of Neo-Gers' 'scores to settle'. How are they going to settle them?

The obvious answer would be through the courts, but Neo-Gers have been unlucky in that respect when it comes to Ashley. Like CJ in *The Fall and Rise of Reginald Perrin*, Ashley didn't get where he is today by being a nice guy. In fact, he's a complete bastard and has built up the resources to take on anybody. He's also taken the precaution of making sure his cases against Neo-Gers are heard in *English* courts. Ashley is well aware of the Masonic culture prevalent in the Scottish justiciary.

So, what the hell are Neo-Gers going to do about their 'enemies'? on the face of it, not a lot. The statements from the likes of John Bennett appear to be just empty threats, made to keep The People happy. As we shall see later, however, those threats might not be so empty after all.

8
I Can't Do Anything

On the 10th of July 2021, Honest Dave appeared in the papers again. He was there to moan about discord among The People. He said,

> I am starting to see the emergence of the type of back-biting by supporters against each other that was so typical and so damaging to the club during the David Murray era.[1]

Surely there wasn't much in the way of dissent during the Murray era. Rangers were winning everything (in Scotland at any rate), Celtic were in the doldrums and nearly went out of business and Rangers were signing top players from England and beyond. The People had never had it so good, and nobody knew about all the cheating yet, even though some suspected. What the hell was Honest Dave on about?

Well, he wasn't going senile yet. There was reason behind the madness. A clue was in another part of his statement.

> I truly hope that the supporter unity that was essential to regime change - and hence our recent success - does not get degraded merely because a few embittered supporters resort to social media as a megaphone to trumpet unfair allegations.[2]

Now, that was a new one. It looked as if he were saying that his Masonic Hall Putsch was a transition from David Murray's reign of terror to his own. This added a whole different dimension to the Big Lie. Craig Whyte, Charles Green and his crew, the Easdales and all the other players in the Neo-Gers saga were being airbrushed out of the story. That would please The People no end, and, by God, King needed to please The People. He wanted their money.

Remember, King had offered his shares to Club 1872 months ago and they hadn't stumped up the cash as yet. They had been given three years to buy his shares for a staggering £13m. They managed to buy some of King's shares at the start of 2021 but announced that any funds raised between then and the summer would go toward investing in the Neo-Gers shares issue that was expected.

> This represents a wonderful opportunity for the Rangers (sic) support to make a massive, multi-million pound, one-off contribution to the financial health of Rangers (sic) whilst also becoming the main custodian of Rangers Football Club (sic) for the first time in its near 150 year history (sic).[3]

Actually, 'multi-million pound' investment was more than a tad ambitious. As it turned out, Club 1872 bought £430,000 worth of shares.[4] Now, although that money could be said to have been invested in Neo-Gers, it wasn't altogether clear where that money would go. Neo-Gers owe Honest Dave a substantial sum for the loans he put into the club. No converting loans into shares for Honest Dave; he wants his money. Speaking of shares, Phil Mac Giolla Bhain believes King is desperate to get his assets out of the UK before Ashley gets everything at Neo-Gers ring-fenced.[5] The question is, which is the more important: getting his loan money back or offloading his shares?

The way King pleaded with The People to keep supporting Club 1872 showed where his priorities lay. It also showed that he was desperately worried about the way things were going. Although he was supposed to have given his blessing to Club 1872's purchase in the share issue,[6] he'd probably have preferred that they used the money to buy some of *his* shares. Besides, the fact that Club 1872 only had £430,000 to spend didn't augur well for their purchase of his shares. The shares were bought from Neo-Gers in April, meaning that was four months' money. A year's money, then, would work out at less than 1½ million. At that rate, Honest Dave would have to wait nine years. No wonder he was trying to drum up more support for Club 1872.

> That (a projected vote of 'no confidence' in the Club 1872 board) is a disservice to all the loyal supporters that supported me at regime change and thereafter.
> Individual share ownership has never been an effective source of supporter influence.
> Club 1872 is the only viable option to achieve that.[7]

This appeal to The People's past unity during the Masonic Hall Putsch was certainly needed. Things weren't going too well at Club 1872. Actually, things had never gone too well at Club 1872. Halloween Houston had baled out in 2017 with no real explanation given, but, apparently, there was all manner of in-fighting going on.[8] This doesn't seem to have abated and has come to a head during the past year, with all kinds of allegations flying about.

In 2020 there were two resignations from the Club 1872 board, Alan Fraser, who nobody has heard of, and Reverend Stuart McQuarrie.[9] You might remember the latter old bigot, who made excuses for The People's vile songbook by indulging in a bit of whatabootery over *The Fields of Athenry*.[10] Some of The People pointed out that MacQuarrie had retired in August 2020 from his post as Chaplain at Glasgow University, so there was nothing untoward going on.[11] Others, however, had a different opinion.

> So The Rangers (sic) Daft Rev has retired and you don't think it would be easier to spend some time on C1872? It's ok for C1872 to demand transparency from the club but they don't give important info like 2 resignations any publicity?
> Had Alan Fraser retired too?
> Something's not right here.[12]

As it turned out, this character was right to be concerned. On May the 19th 2021, Mark Dingwall, of followfollow fame/infamy, announced his intention of standing for one of the two now vacant board places at Club 1872.[13] A week later, he explained why by posting a letter he'd received from Stuart MacQuarrie. It was a pretty lengthy epistle but the gist of it was that MacQuarrie had resigned from the Club 1872 board because, apparently, some of the directors were acting without letting others know what they were up to. The example he gave was a letter written to Castore.[14] One got the impression, though, that there was more to it than that.

The three directors in question were Laura Fawkes, Euan MacFarlane and Joanne Percival.[15] This unholy trinity had seemingly formed a tightly-knit clique, along with someone else that wasn't a board member at all. More about this character later. It's somebody we all know already.

After Mark Dingwall posted Stuart MacQuarrie's letter, things started to move pretty quickly. On the same day, Dingwall told the members of followfollow that he'd been barred from standing for the Club 1872 board. The reasons he was given were twofold:

> 1/ that one, or perhaps more, of my proposers had not been paying for six months continuously into Club 1872.
> 2/ That some of my tweets were "homophobic, ableist, obscene and abusive".[16]

That's a strange one. You'd imagine that somebody that's homophobic, ableist, obscene and abusive would be an ideal person to represent The People! Anyway, the Club 1872 board gave Dingwall five examples of his offensive tweets. In two of them he used the word 'poof,' the others speak for themselves.

> Fuck off you diseased vile cretin.[17]

> Here's an idea Miss Retard - don't show your obsession by following a fan of another in you daft walloper.[18] (Presumably, he meant 'team' rather than 'in'.)

> Away and join Sinn Fein you terroristic cunt![19]

That last comment was directed at Jeremy Corbyn. Again, you could imagine The People voting in droves for somebody coming out with those kinds of statements. Still, they weren't being allowed to by the Unholy Trinity. As usual with anything to do with Neo-Gers and The People hypocrisy was never far away.

Those tweets by Dingwall were from 2016, 2017 and 2019. That doesn't make them any less offensive, but that wasn't where the hypocrisy lay. One commenter on followfollow pointed to where it *did* lie.

> Hasn't stopped another member acting as a shadow director - attending Board meetings, being involved in email rings or being paid by the club. But hey ho.[20]

He didn't say the name, but everyone knew who he meant. It's time to expose that figure, mentioned above, who acted like a director of Club 1872 but wasn't. Introducing Chris 'Listy' Graham. It was Robert Marshall, whose family owns the Louden Taverns on Copland Road and Duke Street, that spilled the beans.

> Chris Graham or his nominee was paid circa £300K by the Club when Dave King was Chairman as a consultant. His job was to basically control Club1872 and make it grow, which retrospectively, looks like it was to get enough money to buy Dave's shares.
> Chris was acting like a shadow Director of Club1872, sat in on meetings and there were no declarations to the Members.
> It is also believed he may have got a company car, although I haven't got that verified.
> One of the most damaging revelations, IMO, is that Club1872 has a Paypal account that, allegedly and I Say allegedly that Chris, even though he is not officially contacted to Club 1872 is in control of this.
> I have it confirmed that some Directors never even knew this Paypal account existed and it was never brought up in their meetings.[21]

This was damning stuff. If that wasn't enough to put The People off giving their money to Club 1872, the fact that Marshall had been interviewed by the police because of some dodgy complaint might well do. The tin hat, though, was put firmly on things when it transpired that Stuart MacQuarrie had been unceremoniously booted out of Club 1872 by the board.[22] After all of that, the internet was full of Huns declaring that they would be leaving Club 1872 and, more importantly, wouldn't be giving them any more money.

Marshall also implicitly pointed up the hypocrisy of not allowing Mark Dingwall to stand for the Club 1872 board. The directors had highlighted Dingwall's historical, offensive tweets yet here they were, hobnobbing with, and possibly even following the orders of, Listy Graham, whose own, well-known, offensive tweet had caused him to be removed from the Neo-Gers board. What was the difference, then, between what Listy had done and what Dingwall had done? It seemed that the Unholy Trinity simply didn't take too well to criticism.

Marshall was trying to call an EGM to get rid of the board and that's when another fact emerged. It turned out that the board hadn't held an AGM for years and ordinary members weren't asked for approval for anything, including the intention of buying Honest Dave's shares.[23] And the rumour mill had even more to say about the board.

It was back in December 2020, when the announcement was made about buying Honest Dave's shares, that Laura Fawkes had to speak out to deny stories that the Unholy Trinity would be pocketing £200,000 apiece when King's shares were finally purchased.[24] Fawkes denied everything, of course, but one particular statement was a cause for doubt.

> We have been very open and clear and transparent about that (the admin assistant, Lil, receiving a salary) since Lil was appointed, which was before my time on the board.[25]

According to Robert Marshall and others on followfollow, the Unholy Trinity wasn't 'open, clear and transparent' about anything! That's why Marshall wanted to clear out the Club 1872 board; to get it back under the control of the members. There was something familiar about all this. It harked back to the days of December 2013 and The Requisitioners. Remember them?

That was the bunch of clowns that thought they could vote out the Neo-Gers board with nothing but a crowd of small shareholders.[26]

There was also a whiff of 2013 when the candidates standing for election to the Club 1872 board were announced. One of them was Malcolm Murray, one of The Requisitioners, who you might remember stoating about pished in that infamous video. He said,

> I have spent a lot of the last nine years trying to bring the people that hurt Rangers (sic) to justice. This has been both costly and dangerous.[27]

It would take more than that piece of generic moaning for Murray to get The People onside. This character had been happy enough to sit on Charles Green's board until he'd been forced out. That would hardly endear him to The People. He was also a reminder of the dark days when Neo-Gers were just starting out in the bottom tier and all the shenanigans that went on back then. There was, too, the embarrassing fact that one of The People's heroes, Walter Smith, had stabbed Malcolm Murray, his friend, in the back.[28] Unsurprisingly, Murray failed to get elected, getting only around 14% of the vote. James Irvine and George Hoggan (No, I don't know either) were voted onto the board.[29]

As yet, there's no sign of a Club 1872 EGM taking place and it looks as if the Unholy Trinity aren't going to be shifted anytime soon. Like anyone else connected with Neo-Gers, however, they're expendable, which they'll discover once Honest Dave has no further use for them. That time might come sooner than they think, especially if things keep going the way they are. Not only are The People deserting Club 1872 in droves, but there's another little problem that might put The People off buying shares altogether.

In June 2017 Club 1872 could boast that it owned 10.71% of the Neo-Gers shares, making it the second-biggest shareholder.[30] By September 2020 that shareholding had dwindled to 6.2%.[31] That had shrunk to 5.1% in June 2021.[32] This meant that Club 1872's stake in Neo-Gers had more than halved in the space of four years, even though, as we have seen, they'd been buying more and more shares. What was the point in continuing to purchase shares just to see the stake-holding percentage keep going down? With Neo-Gers continually having share issues and converting loans into shares, the value of those shares was being constantly diluted; drastically, as we can see. Surely even the low intellects of The People could work out that they'd never have enough shares to get representation on the board.

And that wasn't the only thing that was getting The People riled. The club itself was getting them all worked up as well. It was all to do with MyGers, the Neo-Gers 'loyalty' scheme. It seemed that priority was given to MyGers members when it came to getting tickets. In the current climate, with a limited number going to be allowed into Ibrox, some of The People were fuming at missing out.

> Lot of unrest amongst fans with the my gers scenario, basically it looks like even if you are a ST holder ticked all the boxes yet you wont be considered for 'important' games unless you for(k) out another £45. Rangers (sic) tend to forget where we were 10 years ago when thousands followed and kept the club afloat. To be treated like this is disgracefull, why should any fan be treated differently because they put £45 more into the club? Do we now have a 2 tier fan system depending on how much you can give to the club?[33]

Even those that were members of the scheme weren't happy about the way things were.

> I paid for it and always will for the away games but of course it's a cynical cash grab.[34]

It was called a 'loyalty' scheme, but it looked as if that loyalty only worked one way. As the commenter above said, what about those that had followed Neo-Gers right from the beginning, when they were in the bottom tier? They'd shown their loyalty, but Neo-Gers weren't being very loyal to *them*, unless they were willing to hand over more money.

The problem with MyGers, as many of The People realised, was that handing over £50 each year to be a member wasn't the end of it. Like any loyalty scheme you had to keep making purchases to build up points. Buying 'away' tickets, match programmes, Neo-Gers tops, tat from the shop or online etc. all helped to build up points, just like a Tesco Clubcard. The big difference was that you don't need to pay for a Tesco Clubcard. To many of The People it was simply a con, taking advantage of their much-vaunted loyalty.

On a side note, when you join MyGers you get a welcome pack with a goodie bag. Included in the goodie bag for junior members (they should call them 'Apprentice Members' to be more staunch) is a book called *Learn to Count with Broxi Bear*.[35] This probably isn't endorsed by any educational establishment because it no doubt contains a pull-out number line that goes, '0,55,56,57…'!

Back to the point and there's a bit of a problem with gradually building up points to move up the MyGers tiers. Gold MyGers members have priority when it comes to buying tickets, so how the hell is anybody on Silver meant to buy an 'away' ticket to get more points? It's going to be a perpetual struggle trying to get tickets since the only way to build up points would be to buy multiple replica tops and every piece of crap on sale in the shop. Only those with plenty of money to waste will have any chance of ever getting tickets.

There was even more anger when it was discovered that MyGers members (Gold members, no doubt) were given priority when it came to getting season tickets.[36] Again, the loyalty of those that had always bought season tickets over the years counted for nothing.

> Absolute disgrace from the club if it is mygers getting priority over ST, the club in one hand thanking All ST fans for loyalty and then comes

> BUT we want to squeeze more of you to go on priority list. Unbelievable really.[37]

So, between the nefarious goings-on at Club 1872 and the club itself trying to squeeze them for everything they've got, there were plenty of reasons for dissent among The People. There had to be some way to bring them together. Building metaphorical barricades by telling The People that everyone was against them was all very well, but The People believe that anyway so, although it worked, it had its limitations. Much better was the feel-good factor of winning the league; there have never been so many Neo-Gers tops on display. To keep The People onside, Neo-Gers were going to have to win again. This didn't bode well for the rest of Scottish football.

9
Conscious Consumer

We saw in Chapter 2 how desperate Neo-Gers were for money at the start of season 2020-2021. It was last-chance saloon for them as the vultures were circling. In the season to come, the vultures were still circling, and the bank balance was smaller, if not already in the red. They'd gone through another season spending money they didn't have, and a reckoning was long overdue. That's why they were squeezing The People for everything they had. There was one section of The People that they had so far overlooked; it was time to start getting money out of them too.

The media in Scotland had always had a cosy relationship with Rangers and that had continued with the new club. Of course, there was the odd lovers' tiff, like the BBC refusing to go near Ibrox, but that didn't stop them from still following the party line. It was the printed media, however, that did the most sterling work on Neo-Gers' behalf. In fact, they were essential in keeping The People onside with their 'whatabootery', horror stories about Celtic and feel-good stories about Neo-Gers.

Every year, the Scottish press go through the same rigmarole to convince The People of how lucky they are to have El Guffalo on their team. Each summer, they trot out the same, old, tired tale of some top European team trying to sign the fat oaf. And, of course, the deal always falls through and Neo-Gers are stuck with...er...manage to hold onto him. This year it was Porto that were supposedly interested in him, although why the press thinks we're going to believe this overplayed crap is beyond understanding. The People, though, as we've constantly seen, are more gullible than normal human beings.

There's been a new twist introduced to this banal reportage with the Daily Record claiming that the Portuguese press are responsible for all the Porto stories, with Morelos, apparently, happy to stay at Neo-Gers.[1] That's obviously intended to cheer The People as this much sought-after player wants to stay at their team. Also meant to keep The People happy is this little passage:

> Morelos is due back to Rangers (sic), as scheduled, after his involvement in the Copa America with Colombia.
> Rangers (sic) boss Steven Gerrard has already made it clear that he expects Morelos to be fit and ready to hit the ground running.[2]

Colombia played a total of seven matches in the Copa America tournament, making it to the semi-final and winning the third-place play-off against Peru.[3] Out of all those matches, El Guffalo spent a grand total of nine minutes on the pitch.[4] Never mind being fit and hitting the ground running; he'll need tested for deep-vein thrombosis with all the sitting around he's been doing.

Again, though, The People are gullible and have been led to believe that El Guffalo is their Henrik Larsson. This is the kind of thing the sports media in Scotland excel at, making Neo-Gers look good. For decades now the denizens of the Blue Room have been happy to dole out the succulent lamb and, in some cases, the soup, to these characters for their services. That, however, was about to change. Why should Neo-Gers just hand over their propaganda to the media for free? After all, the agnivores and the soup-takers were members of The People too, weren't they? As such, they were in line to be fleeced as well.

It seemed like a joke, but it was true. The agnivores were going to have to pay for the privilege of being Ibrox cheerleaders. We're not talking about them having to buy their own match tickets here; it was far more substantial than that. Papers were to hand over £25,000, which entitled them to access to Ibrox for one reporter and one photographer to attend matches and pre-match press conferences. Additionally, they'd be entitled to five exclusive interviews and a sit down (whatever the hell *that* is) with Steven Gerrard. A lesser fee of ten grand got you the same access but only *one* exclusive with the manager.⁵

The English media blasted the whole idea but in Scotland, most were strangely quiet about it. It seemed that one paper had already stumped up £25,000. No names were mentioned, but we can all take an educated guess as to which paper it was. Meanwhile, Neo-Gers claimed that 'We are very pleased that we have received positive responses to our media partnership packages.'⁶ Eh? That could only be in Scotland. Only one so-called sports journalist mentioned the deal and didn't seem too happy about it.

Hugh Keevins is persona non grata at Ibrox, but he still probably gets his soup delivered by Meals on Wheels. Or rather, he did. The prospect of the Ibrox soup kitchen closing down had him rattled, so he did what any good agnivore would do; he dragged Celtic into it. His headline said it all, 'Celtic fan conspiracies and Rangers (sic) cash for questions have created awkward atmosphere for new campaign.'⁷

There was no need for Celtic to be dragged into this story except for the usual balancing act of 'one side's as bad as the other.' Of course, Keevins is a bit peeved because he's banned from Celtic Park. That, however, was his own fault for printing lies about the club in his paper.⁸ Whatever his excuse, the fact was that Celtic had no part in this tale and the only reason he had to include them was to suck up to Neo-Gers. Auld Shuggy fair likes his soup!

The People (the ordinary People, minus the agnivores) were divided on the issue of the agnivores having to pay to get into Ibrox. To many of them, it served the press boys bloody well right.

> If they are going write a lot of shite about the club we might as well get paid for it.⁹

> Been profiting off our stories too long. Get yer money out scum.¹⁰

> It could cover legal expenses if the clubs legal counsel has to send a nice letter to discourage inaccurate and slanderous reporting.[11]

> Excellent. I feel Rangers (sic) have given these parasites enough chances to report fairly on them and the press have ignored it every time.[12]

Aw! Bless their wee diabetic socks. They honestly still believe that the Scottish media are against them. This is the thin line that Neo-Gers have chosen to tread, convincing The People that everyone's against them while keeping the agnivores happy. The irony is that the club has relied on the agnivores to perpetuate the myth that the media are against Neo-Gers and The People. One wonders if those agnivores will still be willing accomplices when they have to pay for the privilege.

The People changed their minds about making the press pay when it came to one of their own. Probably everybody's heard of Willie Vass, who's ostensibly a freelance sports photographer but seems to just take pictures at Ibrox. He makes his money by selling his images to newspapers and by selling prints online. He's done this for years, even back when Rangers were still alive. Now, suddenly, he was going to have to pay the same as all the other media. The People, as is their normal reaction, were outraged.[13] One would imagine that Vass, not being interested in exclusive interviews or 'sit downs', would only have to pay £10,000. Even that, however, was too much for The People to stomach.

> Can't believe what I've seen on here today. Willie Vass not getting entry in to Ibrox unless he pays the same money as the gutter establishments that have tarred Rangers (sic) for years. Willie stood by us through all the tough years and shouldn't be treated like this.[14]

As usual, The People had things spectacularly wrong. Vass wasn't doing anybody any favours; he'd been raking in a fortune over the years. He sells his pictures to those very 'gutter establishments' the character above goes on about. He also has a huge archive from which you can buy prints. A standard 8" by 10" will set you back £9.99.[15] This hardly seems worth it since it's no longer like the days when I was a photographer, buggering about in darkrooms with enlargers, filters, acid baths etc. Nowadays, they're just churned out on the Hewlett-Packard from a laptop or even straight from the camera.

As you can imagine, sales to newspapers command much higher prices.[16] He also allows downloads of his images, but not for free and you can bet they won't be ten bob each. So, really, the only difference between this character and the agnivores is that he's been making a lot more money than them.

Anyway, all this bother showed how desperate Neo-Gers were for money. It was going to be a long, hard season having to pay the bills, pay the wages of the players and staff and try to pay Honest Dave back. They needed The People like never before, or, rather, they needed The People's money. As we discussed in the last chapter, the only way they were going to be able to keep The People onside was to win the league again and maybe even add a cup or two.

Despite what had happened last season, Celtic supporters were optimistic. By all accounts, the new manager, Ange Postecoglou, knew what he was doing and demanded exciting, attacking football from his players. He was also, apparently, no 'Yes man' and wouldn't be afraid of standing up to the board if it came to it. The hope was that he'd turn out to be another Brendan Rodgers, who had made a difference to more than a few of the Celtic players. After not being allowed to win last season, the players' confidence was at a low and they needed to believe in themselves again.

Of course, Celtic needed some new players in and Ange (I'm not looking up how to spell that surname every 5 minutes!) had certain targets in mind. The names, however, didn't inspire too much confidence. There was Starfelt, who sounded like a character from some cheesy, 1980s, American science-fiction TV programme such as *Battlestar Galactica*. So did Furuhashi, who conjured up images of the scientist in charge in the likes of *Buck Rogers in the 25th Century*. All we needed was a wee arsehole robot running about shouting, 'Beedy! Beedy!' and we'd have the full set! And as for Soppy... Still, as long as they could do a turn it didn't matter if they were called Hunny McHunface.

Celtic played a few friendlies in England and Wales and showed definite promise. They beat Sheffield Wednesday 3-1 and Charlton Athletic 2-1 and had a creditable 0-0 draw with Bristol City, in which they apparently showed a dominant display.[17] And then they came up against a more formidable opponent. No, not Preston North End, who won the match 1-0, but Kevin Clancy.

Preston's goal came from a penalty, which Celtic diplomatically called 'a soft award'.[18] The truth was that it wasn't a penalty at all. Wasn't it strange that Celtic were doing fine in their matches until they had a Scottish referee in the middle? It was a flag-waving moment; a sign that match officials were going to make sure that their favourite team won again.

More worrying was the friendly against West Ham United on the 24th of July, where Cheatin' Beaton was the referee. Celtic seemed to be holding their own at first and even when West Ham equalised and then scored another to make it 2-1 there still didn't seem too much cause for concern. And then Beaton handed West Ham a penalty. From that point on Celtic simply crumbled. It was like the Celtic of last season, just giving up because they knew they were up against it with Cheatin' Beaton in the middle. There were new signings in the Celtic team, but players talk, and they were no doubt aware of what had happened last season. West Ham ended up winning 6-2.[19]

The score wasn't as concerning as the way Celtic folded. The Daily Record saw it as a worrying sign for the upcoming away game against Midgieland,[20] but there wouldn't be a Scottish referee in charge in Denmark! It certainly didn't bode well for the upcoming league campaign, though.

Conversely, Neo-Gers' only loss among their first three friendlies was when there *wasn't* a Scottish referee in the middle.[21] Then, on the 25th of July, Neo-Gers welcomed Real Madrid to Ibrox. It was a 2-1 victory for Neo-Gers, a victory that the agnivores praised to the heavens.[22] It was notable, though, that Willie Collum was the referee and Neo-Gers didn't score until he'd sent off one of the Real players. Neo-Gers boasted on their website that the two teams might well meet again in the Champions League.[23] Presumably, they were going to be allowed to take their own referees with them and that was why they were so confident!

It looked as if the Widow's Son could rely on a wee bit of help again in the coming season. This, of course, begs the question: will the likes of Brother Boabby and Cheatin' Beaton have to pay to referee at Ibrox? After all, Neo-Gers were looking to gouge everybody among The People, why should the referees be any different?

There was another reason, other than financial, why SFA officials would be helping Neo-Gers to another league win. It was going to look a bit funny if they didn't go all-out to help and Celtic ended up winning the league. What would that say about the 2020-21 season? We all know fine well that Neo-Gers didn't win that league title on their own, but the ones that helped them don't want it exposed for the whole world to see, leaving no doubts. Neo-Gers were going to have to win again to make it look as if, as the agnivores said, they had 'progressed'.

Earlier, on the 14th of July, Celtic announced that they had signed nineteen-year-old Israeli midfielder Liel Abada from Maccabi Petah Tikva F.C. on a five-year deal. The move was, of course, 'subject to international clearance'.[24] Six days later Abada turned out for Celtic in the first leg of their Champions League qualifier against Midgieland. Not only that, but he scored Celtic's only goal in a 1-1 draw.[25] Again, Celtic had impressed and were expected to win the second leg in Denmark the following week. But not if the agnivores had anything to say about it they wouldn't.

The day before the Midgieland game, Clyde Superscoreboard claimed that Abada had been left out of the squad for the match.[26] The Superscoreboard boys probably assumed that Abada had not been included because his 'international clearance' hadn't come through yet. They couldn't believe their eyes when he came out the tunnel at

Celtic Park to take part in the game. When Big Ange took Abada off to replace him with Dane Murray, the Clyde lads thought all their Christmases had come at once. Obviously, Ange had realised his mistake, but it was too late – Celtic had fielded an ineligible player! Auld Hugh Keevins probably pished himself in the excitement.

Normally, the agnivores bang on about coefficients and the like, claiming that we need as many teams as possible to do well in Europe. This is *Sellick* we're talking about, though, so the Superscoreboard boys couldn't wait to grass them up. The match would be declared a 3-0 win for Midgieland, leaving Celtic with an uphill battle. If they lost the away leg, they'd be out of the Champions League before it started and wouldn't be able to drop down into the Europa. Clyde's Andrew Maclean did the honours and was disappointed to discover that they were wrong in their assumptions.

> UEFA confirm Liel Abada's absence from Celtic's squad list ahead of their match against Midtjylland was an IT error on their part.
> The 19-year old had been registered properly by the club.[27]

It turned out that Celtic had taken advantage of being able to register Abada on the Monday night and had done nothing wrong at all. The sense of disappointment and even dismay among the agnivores was almost palpable.[28] What a dirty bunch of bastards, though, to do a thing like that! You can rest assured that they wouldn't have done it if it had been Neo-Gers. And even if it had been Midgieland, they'd have kept their mouths shut and to hell with the coefficients. It showed they were all set for the new season and, even if they weren't prepared to pay to get into Ibrox, they would do all they could to help their favourite club.

Also no doubt ready to help out would be the Scottish Government. Last season they'd been all over Neo-Gers, singling them out for praise for simply doing the same as every other club and turning a blind eye when they didn't. How many times did we hear about 'yellow cards' and 'last chances' without it meaning a thing? Not that Neo-Gers or The People would ever admit it. According to them, the SNP, in common with just about everyone else, had it in for them.

An example of how the SNP were against them was when both Neo-Gers and Celtic would be playing friendlies on the same day. As the Daily Record put it,

> Celtic will welcome 18,500 fans to their clash with West Ham while less than half of that will be in attendance at Ibrox later that day.[29]

Glasgow Council explained that they were acting in accordance with an agreement with Scotland's Safety Advisory Group, in which crowds were to be gradually increased. This was to occur after Scotland went to Level 0 on the 19th of July. Celtic had played Midgieland on the 20th in front of a crowd of 9,000, which they were allowed to double for their *second* game. Neo-Gers would be playing their *first* match after Level 0 was declared on the 24th, in front of 8,500 and would be allowed to double the crowd for their *second* match, which was to take place the very next day.[30] The People, however, couldn't get their heads round that one.

> Dirty lying Scumbags.[31]
>
> Pish.[32]
>
> They don't even try to hide it.[33]

Neo-Gers were just as bad, with claims that the board wasn't happy about the situation.

> They simply cannot understand why Glasgow City Council are only allowing them to welcome in 8,500 fans to Ibrox when there will be double that at Parkhead for a game kicking-off two hours before. It just doesn't make sense.[34]

Well, it wouldn't make sense, would it? For anything to make sense requires a certain amount of brain cells, which seem to be in short supply at Ibrox. One thing that *does* make sense is The People follow-following this particular club. It's a case of the blind leading the blind or, rather, the thick leading the thick.

No prizes for guessing why the Neo-Gers board wanted as many bodies as possible entering Ibrox, which is where we came in. As mentioned earlier, there were still plenty of folk waiting the chance to get money out of Neo-Gers; money that Neo-Gers didn't have. Nobody knew when the courts' backlogs would be cleared and Mike Ashley and the rest would swoop, so Neo-Gers had to be ready. No wonder they were trying to scrape together as much money as they could get. Before the season's over they'll probably start charging clubs for their teams to play on the hallowed turf at Ibrox. Or maybe they could charge clubs for Neo-Gers playing at their grounds and bringing more paying customers in. After all, we all know that the Blue Pound is the only thing keeping Scotland afloat!

10
The Day The World Turned Day-Glo

Since this is the last book in the series, it's fitting that we look at what the future holds for Neo-Gers. In the last chapter, we looked at the immediate future, which is going to be all about the vultures descending to tear apart Neo-Gers' rotting carcass. As we have learned, though, that doesn't mean the end. If we look years, or even decades, ahead there'll still be a club stinking up the place that The People, the agnivores and the football authorities call 'Rangers'. We might as well accept it.

Those expecting another liquidation event and a new incarnation of 'Rangers' – Neo-Gers 2, The The Rangers or whatever – are going to be sadly disappointed. Yes, a liquidation event is almost inevitable but this time around there *is* a holding company, the Sooper-Dooper Intergalactic Football Club PLC.[1] The club itself has a separate board, though who sits on it is anybody's guess. So, if things do go tits-up, it'll be the holding company that'll be liquidated, not the club. The fact that this model was put in place almost immediately when Charlie Green set up his new club showed that lessons had been learned. That such a model didn't exist before proves that Rangers did, in fact, die. That, however, is scant consolation for the knowledge that we might never be rid of the bastards!

Liquidation might come sooner rather than later since it's the only way they're going to get rid of Mike Ashley. All contracts are with the Sooper-Dooper Intergalactic Football Club PLC, so if that dies, then so do the contracts. Ashley's, and everybody else's, court cases would then be a waste of time and money. Meanwhile, a phoenix company could buy the holding company's only asset: Neo-Gers FC. It would be a risky procedure and would have to involve a tame, compliant administrator or liquidator, a firm like Duff and Phelps. It could well be worth it, though, especially since it looks as if Ashley is still closely linked with Neo-Gers.

We saw earlier that there have been persistent rumours of Ashley being involved in Castore. Those rumours took wings when it was announced that Castore was the new kit supplier for Newcastle United.[2] Why would Ashley allow these upstarts in unless there was something in it for him? The fact that all Castore kits were available in Sports Direct stores only increased the speculation.[3] The People wouldn't be best pleased if these rumours turned out to be true.

Of course, The People wouldn't be too happy either if the Sooper-Dooper Intergalactic Football Club PLC was liquidated. It would mean they'd lose all their MyGers points and any money they put into the Temple of Doom. And Club 1872's dwindling percentage of ownership of Neo-Gers would disappear as well. Not that The People would be too upset about that; by that time they wouldn't be putting money into that bottomless pit anyway.

As we all know, however, there are no more gullible folk on the planet than The People and they wouldn't be angry or upset for very long. As long as there was still a team they could follow-follow they'd be perfectly willing to accept that the new, phoenix holding company had 'saved Raynjurz'.

The People were going to have other things to keep them angry and upset. You might remember that most of them refused to support their home nation in the Euros, preferring to support England. That didn't work out too well for them, but it had nothing to do with how the England team performed. Perversely, it was the integrity of the England team that got them all bamboozled.

The English Brexiteers, remember, booed their own players when they 'took the knee' against racism. It drove them almost demented when the team refused to stop doing it. They were nearly apoplectic when England lost to Italy in the final via a penalty shoot-out. Their racial hatred boiled over when it finally dawned on them that the three penalty misses had been made by black players.

Those three players were deluged with racist abuse online by English gammons. Boris Johnson and other Tories condemned the abuse and blamed social media companies.[4] It wasn't long before everyone pointed out the hypocrisy of Johnson and his fellow Tories, who had refused to condemn the booing of the players, effectively condoning racism. A reception for the players at 10 Downing Street had to be cancelled, ostensibly because Johnson was busy, but it soon emerged that the players had refused to attend because of the way Johnson had encouraged racism.[5]

That level of integrity seriously disturbed England's Brexity types and, consequently, The People as well. We already know what The People's attitude to taking the knee is and their racism is legendary, so, obviously, they were on the side of those bigoted Brexiteers. They wouldn't have a lot of sympathy with Marcus Rashford either because he's a bit…well…*lefty*, isn't he? Just like the Tories and other English right-wingers, they put the blame on social media.[6]

To the English gammons, the England team had become *anti*-English and you can be damned sure that The People felt the same way, although they'd prefer the term *anti-British*. This is the dilemma they're faced with. They normally support England because of the Queen, hating the SNP, being Unionists, supporting the 'archetypal British team' etc. etc. But now it seemed that the England football team was in opposition to all that The People stood for. What were they to do? It was enough to make their heads explode! Still, there's always the Northern Ireland team.

Speaking of Northern Ireland, The People over there are long used to getting their own way about practically everything. By means of threats and intimidation, Loyalist gangs make sure the authorities acquiesce. Of course, it helps that they have plenty of sympathetic ears in the police, local councils and at Stormont.

A prime example of how they get their own way is the annual bigotfest they hold on the 11th of July each year. They build huge 'bonefires' that tower above nearby houses. Instead of stopping these fires from occurring, the police evacuate the houses and the local council boards them up. Once the conflagration is started, the fire brigade turns up. They don't put out the fire, though. Instead, they hose down the houses in the hope that this will stop them catching fire. This insane drama takes place annually and it's a miracle that nobody's been seriously injured or even killed. It's only a matter of time.

As we all know, The People have plenty of sympathisers in Scotland as well, in the police, the judiciary, the media and even in politics. In 2021, they decided that it was time to take a leaf out of their Northern Irish brethren's book. On the 15th of May, a briefing from Police Scotland to the Scottish Government said,

> The Rangers (sic) risk group known as the Union Bears requested police to facilitate a mass procession threatening a 'riot' if this request was not granted.[7]

The briefing went on, saying, 'The request was denied and engagement continued.'[8] So why, then, did the police do exactly what the Union Bears had demanded? No effort was made to disperse the crowds outside Ibrox, and the police escorted them all the way to George Square in what looked like a guard of honour. No effort was made either to guide the mob to a park or some other place where they would cause less trouble. It seemed as if the Union Bears' threats had paid off.

It's unclear if this tactic had been attempted before, but it was a worrying sign. There is a phrase that's been doing the rounds for a while now, started by Tories and lapped up eagerly by The People. It's that of the 'Ulsterisation of Scottish politics.' As one Tory put it,

> The SNP has sought to ally itself and its people with the Irish nationalist cause and has attempted to draw parallels between the two situations. Tactics straight out of the Sinn Fein playbook should concern people across the political spectrum in Scotland and the wider United Kingdom.[9]

Now, that was a complete load of shite. Nobody in the SNP has allied it with Irish nationalists, whether Sinn Fein or anyone else. That's all in the minds of The People and their sympathisers. The real Ulsterisation of Scottish politics came when The People and their ilk voted tactically to keep the SNP out. Politics in Scotland has become polarised over a single issue and it's not the SNP to blame. It's the Tories that have been banging on about the Union, getting The People on their side.[10] They've even resurrected the old name of 'Unionist' that had died out about forty years ago.

Now a new element has been added. With The People aware that they can get their own way with threats, how long will it be before we start having 'bonefires' in Scotland? The People in Scotland would be perfectly happy to have fires burning night and day, turning the whole sky a bright shade of orange. Hopefully, it doesn't come to this, but we can't count on the SNP to stop them. As we've seen, they've been going out of their way to suck up to The People and there's no reason to believe that's going to change anytime soon.

Back to Neo-Gers themselves and we've already noted how it's in the Establishment's interests for the Ibrox club to win again in season 2021-22. Things might well go much further than that, though. Celtic's nine titles in a row of the 1960s and 1970s is often forgotten in the rush to praise Rangers' cheats for achieving the same record. In fact, the agnivores often give the impression that the Huns did it first and it was their record alone. Now that Celtic have done it twice, what are the chances that all the stops will be pulled out to even the score?

Of course, any normal person knows that Rangers can't win any more titles because they're dead. But the Big Lie insists that they're still alive and playing out of Ibrox. So, the stage is set for things to be evened up with 'Rangers' winning a 'second' nine in a row. That means suffering The People being triumphant and destroying George Square every year from now until 2029. It doesn't bear thinking about, does it?

I'm painting a pretty gloomy picture here, but then again, maybe I'm totally wrong in my predictions. (Here's hoping!) Perhaps Big Ange is the kick up the arse that Celtic need and we'll get our title back at the end of this coming season. The odds, however, as well as the football authorities, the Scottish

Government, the media and possibly even the Celtic board, are stacked against us. It'll be a hard fight, but it could be done.

Hopefully, we'll see Celtic back at the top and we can go back to laughing at the Huns. At the moment, all we've got are the memories; but what memories they are. Don't worry, I'm not going to recount them all here. If you want to relive those halcyon days, I can recommend seven other books for you to read!

NOTES

Introduction

[1] https://philmacgiollabhain.ie/2020/08/25/the-real-castore-story-is-being-ignored-by-the-stenography-corps/#more-17842

[2] https://philmacgiollabhain.ie/2020/08/01/ashley-still-in-the-game-at-ibrox/#more-17567

[3] https://www.dailyrecord.co.uk/sport/football/football-news/rangers-lift-veolia-trophy-james-22378648

[4] https://www.thescottishsun.co.uk/sport/football/5828372/celtic-chris-sutton-rangers-veolia-trophy/

[5] https://www.bbc.co.uk/sport/football/53516778

[6] ibid

[7] https://timesofmalta.com/articles/view/lask-linz-deducted-points-for-covid-19-rules-breach.795238

[8] https://www.edinburghnews.scotsman.com/sport/football/hibs/hibs-regret-covid-19-test-delay-they-apologise-fuming-ross-county-over-cancelled-friendly-2919454

[9] https://www.thescottishsun.co.uk/sport/football/5848484/rangers-dundee-united-no-linesmen/

[10] https://www.thescottishsun.co.uk/sport/football/5847276/rangers-sfa-probe-nine-players-testing/

[11] https://www.dailyrecord.co.uk/sport/football/football-news/rangers-motherwell-hibs-escape-sfa-22463659

[12] Ibid

Chapter 1

[1] https://www.bbc.co.uk/sport/football/53535016

[2] https://www.bbc.co.uk/sport/football/53541535

[3] https://www.skysports.com/watch/video/sports/football/competitions/scottish-premiership/12040484/red-card-for-considine

[4] https://www.skysports.com/football/hibernian-vs-rangers/report/425610

[5] https://www.bbc.co.uk/sport/football/54135422

[6] https://www.bbc.co.uk/sport/football/54222424

[7] https://www.followfollow.com/forum/threads/rangers-twitter-should-call-out-stewart.135380/

[8] https://www.followfollow.com/forum/threads/sport-scene-surprise-surprise.135236/

[9] ibid

[10] https://paddyontherailway.wordpress.com/2020/09/30/pat-mick-and-the-irishman/

[11] https://www.followfollow.com/forum/threads/gers-penalty-calls-against-

motherwell-defended-by-ex-referee-hugh-dallas.135368/
[12] https://www.followfollow.com/forum/threads/sport-scene-surprise-surprise.135236/
[13] https://www.bbc.co.uk/sport/football/54290324
[14] https://www.youtube.com/watch?v=3ia36TrO5_8
[15] https://www.bbc.co.uk/sport/football/54679336
[16] https://www.bbc.co.uk/sport/football/54766673
[17] https://www.bbc.co.uk/sport/football/54948346
[18] https://www.bbc.co.uk/sport/football/55373709
[19] https://www.glasgowtimes.co.uk/sport/19224347.joe-newell-need-get-punched-head-get-penalty-ibrox---hibs-can-beat-rangers/?ref=rss
[20] https://www.dailyrecord.co.uk/sport/football/football-news/jim-goodwin-calls-rangers-referee-23236481
[21] https://www.dailyrecord.co.uk/sport/football/football-news/dermot-gallagher-rangers-penalty-acquittal-23229503
[22] https://www.bbc.co.uk/sport/football/55373709
[23] https://www.dailyrecord.co.uk/sport/football/football-news/steven-gerrards-rangers-discipline-assessment-23161953
[24] https://www.bbc.co.uk/sport/football/55204189
[25] https://www.bbc.co.uk/sport/football/55294879
[26] https://www.rangers.co.uk/article/rangers-earn-battling-victory-against-dundee-united/5BOP17MODqXvYP6uJz3NqK
[27] https://www.dailyrecord.co.uk/sport/football/football-news/alfredo-morelos-discover-fate-rangers-23167555
[28] https://www.bbc.co.uk/sport/football/55323209
[29] https://www.bbc.co.uk/sport/football/55450349
[30] https://www.bbc.co.uk/sport/football/55516866
[31] ibid
[32] https://www.youtube.com/watch?v=R-24T0U0PyI
[33] https://twitter.com/RangersFC/status/1356564489420865537
[34] https://www.youtube.com/watch?v=ODu8xHCL0Xg
[35] https://www.dailyrecord.co.uk/sport/football/football-news/steven-gerrard-hits-out-sfa-23426865
[36] https://www.dailyrecord.co.uk/sport/football/football-news/kemar-roofe-rangers-tackle-receives-23439953
[37] https://www.youtube.com/watch?v=aQX1vOrHP5o
[38] https://www.dailyrecord.co.uk/sport/football/football-news/steven-gerrard-ramps-up-rangers-23488041
[39] https://www.dailyrecord.co.uk/sport/football/football-news/rangers-slams-sfa-disciplinary-process-23479739
[40] https://www.youtube.com/watch?v=fukhl4el4S8
[41] https://www.dailyrecord.co.uk/sport/football/football-news/ryan-hedges-rangers-red-card-23294283
[42] https://www.bbc.co.uk/sport/football/56477199
[43] https://www.youtube.com/watch?v=sTa9t3ypCgE
[44] https://www.youtube.com/watch?v=Z_rHtH6DUFw
[45] https://www.youtube.com/watch?v=XUckM3XBSO4

[46] https://www.bbc.co.uk/sport/football/56564088
[47] https://www.youtube.com/watch?v=XUckM3XBSO4
[48] https://www.bbc.co.uk/sport/football/55031989
[49] https://www.dailyrecord.co.uk/sport/football/football-news/betfred-cup-draw-live-rangers-23087793
[50] https://www.stmirren.com/home-matchday-information/3854-up-next-st-mirren-v-rangers-16th-december
[51] https://www.bbc.co.uk/sport/football/47011430
[52] https://www.bbc.co.uk/sport/football/53626123
[53] https://www.skysports.com/football/st-mirren-vs-rangers/report/440122
[54] https://www.bbc.co.uk/sport/live/football/55288268/page/2
[55] http://mysongbook.de/msb/songs/f/footbref.html
[56] https://www.dailyrecord.co.uk/sport/football/football-news/ref-steven-mclean-embarrassing-alan-5563222
[57] https://www.followfollow.com/forum/threads/alan-muir-today%E2%80%99s-hapless-idiot.146194/page-2
[58] https://celticnoise.com/threads/we-can-all-use-a-laugh.6425/page-135
[59] https://worldreferee.com/referee/alan_muir/#:~:text=Alan%20Muir%20was%20a%20UEFA%20Category%203%20referee,2011%20when%20he%20was%20off%20the%20FIFA%20panel.
[60] https://www.followfollow.com/forum/threads/how-did-they-keep-11-men-on-the-park.162411/
[61] ibid
[62] ibid
[63] ibid
[64] https://www.youtube.com/watch?v=ktojxK-cTZE
[65] https://www.bbc.co.uk/sport/football/56789585

Chapter 2

[1] https://www.skysports.com/football/news/11095/12279788/european-super-league-the-key-questions-what-is-it-who-is-involved-how-likely
[2] https://www.thesun.co.uk/sport/football/14896592/prem-uefa-money-european-super-league/
[3] https://fanbanter.co.uk/current-debt-of-all-12-european-super-league-clubs-makes-for-shocking-reading/
[4] https://www.thesun.co.uk/sport/football/14896592/prem-uefa-money-european-super-league/
[5] https://www.forbes.com/sites/samindrakunti/2019/12/28/crashing-down-a-decade-of-corruption-cripples-fifa/?sh=6ebcd06cd450
[6] https://www.sportekz.com/football/scottish-premiership-prize-money/#:~:text=TV%20money%20will%20be%20the%20key-factor%20in%20future,League%201%2C%20league%202%20and%20Championship%20division%20teams.
[7] https://www.bbc.co.uk/sport/football/43002985
[8] https://www.dailyrecord.co.uk/sport/football/football-news/scottish-footballs-biggest-transfers-the-9691792

[9] http://www.midfielddynamo.com/transfers/list_recordfees.htm
[10] https://twitter.com/Heavidor/status/1392163670726164493
[11] https://www.ukbusinessforums.co.uk/threads/true-cost-of-photocopying.66784/
[12] https://www.bbc.co.uk/sport/football/55151773
[13] https://www.dailyrecord.co.uk/sport/football/football-news/dave-king-issues-200m-rangers-23117333
[14] https://www.bbc.co.uk/sport/football/55321442
[15] https://www.rangersnews.uk/news/championship-stars-35m-valuation-must-serve-as-warning-to-rangers/
[16] https://www.thescottishsun.co.uk/sport/football/7065795/rangers-administrators-56-8m-bonkers-bdo-strategy-shut-down/
[17] https://www.heraldscotland.com/news/19278678.ex-rangers-administrators-fight-bonkers-56-8m-shut-club-down-claim/
[18] https://www.thescottishsun.co.uk/sport/football/7065795/rangers-administrators-56-8m-bonkers-bdo-strategy-shut-down/
[19] https://rangers.vitalfootball.co.uk/rangers-administration-liquidation/
[20] https://www.dailyrecord.co.uk/news/scottish-news/top-cop-behind-rangers-fraud-23908311
[21] https://www.thescottishsun.co.uk/news/6662145/rangers-crown-office-lord-advocate-malicious-prosecution/
[22] https://scottishlegal.com/article/malicious-prosecution-scandal-duff-and-phelps-sues-lord-advocate-for-25m
[23] https://www.theguardian.com/uk/1999/oct/19/davidpallister1
[24] https://www.inflationtool.com/british-pound/1995-to-present-value
[25] https://www.67hailhail.com/news/report-petty-rivals-banned-celtic-pundit-for-comments-on-their-financial-situation/
[26] https://www.followfollow.com/forum/threads/pathetic-quality-on-castores-rfc-range-updated-post-4-915-%E2%80%93-my-football-shirts-are-falling-to-pieces.131069/
[27] https://www.glasgowtimes.co.uk/news/19337793.rangers-lose-right-2-8m-merchandise-income-due-mike-ashley-legal-block/?ref=rss
[28] https://www.thesun.co.uk/sport/football/14986187/sheffield-united-mcburnie-out-scotland-euro-2020/
[29] https://talksport.com/football/878916/sheffield-united-twitter-video-oli-mcburnie-news-punch-fight/
[30] https://www.thescottishsun.co.uk/sport/football/3804691/rangers-daft-oli-mcburnie-refuses-huddle-swansea/
[31] https://www.dailyrecord.co.uk/sport/football/football-news/oli-mcburnie-john-fleck-huddle-23459597
[32] https://www.dailyrecord.co.uk/sport/football/football-transfer-news/oli-mcburnie-linked-rangers-career-24201151?utm_source=twitter.com&utm_medium=social&utm_campaign=sharebar
[33] https://www.dailymail.co.uk/sport/football/article-9626837/Rangers-pursue-15m-Sheffield-United-striker-Oli-McBurnie.html
[34] https://www.msn.com/en-gb/sport/american-football/fresh-rangers-

transfer-update-emerges-on-c2-a3171m-rated-ace-who-gerrard-dubbed-outstanding/ar-AAL9uZk?ocid=uxbndlbing
[35]https://www.glasgowtimes.co.uk/sport/19341389.rangers-launch-6-75m-share-issue-fans-invest-pivotal-moment-history/?ref=twtrec
[36] ibid
[37]https://videocelts.com/2021/06/blogs/latest-news/scottish-government-and-their-3-2m-ibrox-bail-out/
[38]https://www.glasgowlive.co.uk/sport/rangers-give-fans-glimpse-new-20664161
[39]https://www.rangers.co.uk/Article/official-supporter-packages-for-edmiston-house/1umYG054cX5qrhMPwTML0H
[40] ibid
[41]https://www.glasgowlive.co.uk/news/glasgow-news/rangers-ibrox-flats-albion-car-18285635
[42]https://www.dailyrecord.co.uk/news/scottish-news/rangers-shares-held-criminal-firm-13670278
[43] https://celticnoise.com/threads/ibrox-money-laundering-operation.4599/
[44] https://twitter.com/Heavidor/status/1392163670726164493

Chapter 3

[1] https://www.bbc.co.uk/sport/football/53535016
[2]https://www.dailyrecord.co.uk/news/scottish-news/aberdeen-players-pictured-night-out-22484167
[3] ibid
[4] https://www.bbc.co.uk/news/business-54015221
[5]https://metro.co.uk/2020/10/30/eat-out-to-help-out-coronavirus-13508814/#:~:text=Eat%20Out%20to%20Help%20Out%20was%20a%20scheme,visit%20restaurants%20accelerated%20the%20rate%20of%20coronavirus%20infections,
[6]https://www.thenational.scot/news/18630299.aberdeen-lockdown-32-locations-linked-covid-19-cluster/
[7]https://www.thescottishsun.co.uk/sport/football/5905415/aberdeen-covid-19-pub-identities-silence-apologise/
[8] https://www.bbc.co.uk/sport/football/53626123
[9] https://www.bbc.co.uk/sport/football/53626124
[10] https://www.youtube.com/watch?v=RMhvDrUx9d0
[11] https://www.bbc.co.uk/sport/football/53626124
[12]https://www.dailymail.co.uk/sport/sportsnews/article-8613671/Scottish-football-season-HALTED-Celtic-defender-Boli-Bolingoli-travelled-Spain.html
[13] ibid
[14]https://www.thescottishsun.co.uk/news/scottish-news/5912833/celtic-bolingoli-spain-quarantine-coronavirus/#comments
[15] ibid (comments section)
[16] ibid
[17]https://www.thescottishsun.co.uk/sport/football/5914793/nicola-sturgeon-celtic-aberdeen-bolingoli-aberdeen/

[18] https://www.bbc.co.uk/sport/football/53729449
[19] ibid
[20] https://www.thescottishsun.co.uk/sport/football/5908436/aberdeen-celtic-hamilton-postponed-kris-boyd/
[21] https://www.thescottishsun.co.uk/sport/football/5931819/celtic-forfeit-points-bolingoli-covid-19-cancelled-boyd/
[22] https://www.bbc.co.uk/sport/football/54235095
[23] https://www.dailyrecord.co.uk/sport/football/football-news/rangers-title-jolt-boli-bolingolis-22503910
[24] https://www.dailyrecord.co.uk/news/scottish-news/celtic-star-boli-bolingoli-pictured-22503741
[25] ibid
[26] https://www.thescottishsun.co.uk/sport/football/5914793/nicola-sturgeon-celtic-aberdeen-bolingoli-aberdeen/
[27] https://www.followfollow.com/forum/threads/bolingolis-trip-to-spain-new-evidence.134834/
[28] ibid
[29] https://www.followfollow.com/forum/threads/bolingolis-trip-to-spain-new-evidence.134834/page-2
[30] https://www.followfollow.com/forum/threads/bolingolis-trip-to-spain-new-evidence.134834/page-3
[31] https://twitter.com/VanguardBears/status/1293173496994988037
[32] https://www.thescottishsun.co.uk/sport/football/5931819/celtic-forfeit-points-bolingoli-covid-19-cancelled-boyd/
[33] https://www.bbc.co.uk/sport/football/54290322
[34] https://www.dailyrecord.co.uk/sport/football/football-news/odsonne-edouard-blow-celtic-striker-22804053
[35] https://www.dailyrecord.co.uk/sport/football/football-news/nir-bitton-adds-celtic-covid-22824950
[36] https://www.scottishfa.co.uk/news/scottish-fa-confirms-positive-covid-19-case-in-scotland-squad/?rid=13925
[37] ibid
[38] https://www.premierleague.com/match/58936
[39] https://www.dailyrecord.co.uk/sport/football/football-news/ryan-christie-celtic-return-hope-22853598
[40] https://www.dailyrecord.co.uk/sport/football/football-news/ryan-christies-celtic-vs-rangers-22811762
[41] https://www.dailyrecord.co.uk/sport/football/football-news/every-celtic-player-must-quarantine-22812546
[42] https://www.justarsenal.com/great-news-tierney-cleared-to-play-against-man-city/261172
[43] https://www.premierleague.com/match/58941
[44] https://www.glasgowlive.co.uk/sport/football/football-news/celtic-rangers-christie-tierney-arsenal-19114374
[45] https://www.dailyrecord.co.uk/news/scottish-news/rangers-players-jordan-jones-george-22944313
[46] https://www.dailyrecord.co.uk/sport/football/football-news/jordan-jones-

george-edmundson-face-22943770
[47] https://twitter.com/ScotsIrishCelt/status/1323264617217466373
[48] https://sentinelcelts.com/2020/11/05/hes-in-the-sock-drawer/
[49] https://www.rangersnews.uk/columnist/celtic-fans-mental-covid-conspiracy-claims-show-what-rangers-are-up-against/
[50] https://www.thescottishsun.co.uk/news/scottish-news/6231171/rangers-jordan-jones-george-edmunson-party-fine-coronavirus-pics/
[51] ibid
[52] https://www.thescottishsun.co.uk/sport/football/6231336/jones-edmundson-rangers-careers-over-kris-boyd/
[53] https://www.dailyrecord.co.uk/sport/football/football-news/jordan-jones-george-edmundson-hit-22959296
[54] https://www.glasgowtimes.co.uk/sport/18883745.rangers-pair-george-edmundson-jordan-jones-handed-seven-match-bans/
[55] https://www.dailyrecord.co.uk/sport/football/football-news/scottish-government-commend-rangers-jordan-22946093
[56] https://punditarena.com/football/daniel-hussey/celtic-dubai/
[57] https://www.glasgowlive.co.uk/sport/football/football-news/every-word-neil-lennons-celtic-19651698
[58] https://www.caughtoffside.com/2021/01/05/these-celtic-fans-are-furious-after-images-of-pints-at-poolside-emerge-from-clubs-dubai-trip/
[59] https://www.thescottishsun.co.uk/news/scottish-news/6494482/celtic-dubai-pictures-nicola-sturgeon-social-distancing/
[60] https://punditarena.com/football/daniel-hussey/celtic-dubai/
[61] https://www.dailymail.co.uk/sport/sportsnews/article-9113913/Holyrood-call-SFA-investigate-Celtics-controversial-Dubai-training-camp.html
[62] https://thecelticfamily.wordpress.com/2021/01/20/when-your-instinct-tells-you-its-true-go-with-it/
[63] ibid
[64] https://www.glasgowlive.co.uk/sport/football/football-news/every-word-neil-lennons-celtic-19651698
[65] https://www.celticquicknews.co.uk/3m-rule-for-celtic-only-farrygate-but-from-the-government-this-time/?utm_source=dlvr.it&utm_medium=twitter
[66] https://www.thescottishsun.co.uk/sport/football/6277048/watch-scotland-stars-conga-david-marshall/
[67] ibid
[68] https://thecelticblog.com/2021/01/articles-and-features/another-celtic-player-tests-positive-and-the-media-instantly-starts-the-blame-game/
[69] https://www.dailyrecord.co.uk/sport/football/football-news/neil-lennon-13-celtic-players-23297518
[70] https://www.bbc.co.uk/sport/football/55708291
[71] https://metro.co.uk/2021/04/04/kate-garraway-says-second-easter-without-husband-derek-is-so-hard-14355824/
[72] https://www.channel4.com/press/news/dispatches-uncovers-serious-failings-one-uks-largest-covid-testing-labs
[73] https://www.bbc.co.uk/news/uk-56556806
[74] https://www.theguardian.com/world/2020/nov/15/chumocracy-covid-

revealed-shape-tory-establishment
[75] https://www.flyhighfitness.org/olympics-2021-preparations/
[76] https://www.independent.co.uk/news/uk/politics/stanley-johnson-boris-greece-foreign-office-travel-restriction-a9597401.html
[77] https://www.glasgowlive.co.uk/sport/football/football-news/every-word-neil-lennons-celtic-19651698
[78] https://www.dailyrecord.co.uk/news/scottish-news/rangers-investigating-claims-players-breach-23500618
[79] https://www.dailyrecord.co.uk/sport/football/football-news/rangers-handed-step-back-warning-23506264
[80] https://www.dailyrecord.co.uk/sport/football/football-news/steven-gerrard-names-5-rangers-23516275
[81] https://www.bbc.co.uk/sport/football/56138759
[82] https://www.bbc.co.uk/sport/football/56054515#tab-Line-ups
[83] ibid
[84] https://www.bbc.co.uk/sport/football/56138759
[85] ibid
[86] https://www.kickoff.com/news/articles/world-news/categories/news/sa-players-abroad/bongani-zungu-steven-gerrard-defends-treatment-of-bafana-bafana-star-and-other-covid-offenders/695385
[87] https://www.dailyrecord.co.uk/sport/football/football-news/steven-gerrard-names-5-rangers-23516275
[88] https://twitter.com/bimmerbhoy/status/1362420563940159488
[89] https://www.dailyrecord.co.uk/sport/football/football-news/every-word-steven-gerrards-rangers-23516494
[90] https://www.bbc.co.uk/sport/football/53951005?intlink_from_url=
[91] https://www.glasgowtimes.co.uk/sport/18883745.rangers-pair-george-edmundson-jordan-jones-handed-seven-match-bans/
[92] https://www.dailyrecord.co.uk/sport/football/football-news/rangers-respond-covid-5-hit-23823218
[93] https://www.glasgowlive.co.uk/sport/football/football-news/rangers-appeal-bans-after-covid-20314014
[94] https://www.glasgowtimes.co.uk/news/19219849.scottish-fa-set-date-rangers-five-covid-appeal-hearing/
[95] https://www.bbc.co.uk/sport/football/56178096
[96] https://www.dailyrecord.co.uk/sport/football/football-news/rangers-receive-rapturous-ibrox-welcome-23619440
[97] https://www.bbc.co.uk/sport/football/56219996
[98] https://www.dailyrecord.co.uk/sport/football/football-news/rangers-kick-title-party-heading-23620779
[99] https://www.dailyrecord.co.uk/sport/football/football-news/inside-rangers-dressing-room-stars-23621316
[100] https://www.dailyrecord.co.uk/sport/football/football-news/alfredo-morelos-toasts-rangers-win-23620993
[101] https://twitter.com/Tam_Selleck/status/1368330138165911552
[102] ibid
[103] https://www.dailyrecord.co.uk/news/scottish-news/footage-rangers-

players-allegedly-singing-24124010
[104] https://www.youtube.com/watch?v=d2q2FFumob4
[105] https://twitter.com/JFaeTheYY/status/1394711141209706498
[106] https://www.msn.com/en-gb/news/newsscotland/footage-of-rangers-fc-stars-partying-in-plush-scots-pad-probed-by-cops/ar-BB1gSdHe?ocid=msedgntp
[107] https://twitter.com/JFaeTheYY/status/1394711141209706498

Chapter 4

[1] https://www.dailyrecord.co.uk/sport/football/football-news/fergus-mccanns-battle-save-celtic-3013568

[2] http://celticunderground.net/murky-world-of-murray-and-masterton/

[3] https://thecelticstar.com/celtics-transfer-strategy-and-the-champions-league-failures-coming-home-to-roost/

[4] https://www.dailyrecord.co.uk/sport/football/football-news/neil-lennon-fate-fears-under-23088571

[5] https://www.dailyrecord.co.uk/news/scottish-news/shocking-scenes-outside-parkhead-fans-23088971

[6] https://www.dailyrecord.co.uk/sport/football/football-news/disgusted-ally-mccoist-slaughters-celtic-23089944

[7] https://www.dailymail.co.uk/sport/football/article-2914175/Sack-board-Rangers-fans-storm-Ibrox-match-Hearts-postponed.html

[8] https://philmacgiollabhain.ie/2020/12/02/celtics-sycophancy-problem-in-the-boardroom/#more-19160

[9] https://www.dailyrecord.co.uk/sport/football/football-news/peter-lawwells-every-celtic-word-23165456

[10] https://www.dailyrecord.co.uk/sport/football/football-news/charlie-nicholas-stark-rangers-money-23296082

[11] https://www.dailyrecord.co.uk/sport/football/football-news/andy-walker-fillets-arrogant-celtic-23300833

[12] https://www.dailyrecord.co.uk/sport/football/football-news/andy-walker-hammers-celtic-over-23445995

[13] https://www.dailymail.co.uk/sport/football/article-9206795/Neil-Lennon-lays-players-Celtic-lose-home-St-Mirren-time-30-YEARS.html

[14] https://www.bbc.co.uk/sport/football/56390446

[15] https://www.bbc.co.uk/sport/football/56873186

[16] https://www.dailyrecord.co.uk/sport/football/football-news/neil-lennon-leaves-celtic-live-23554859

[17] https://www.dailymail.co.uk/sport/football/article-9200629/Celtic-chief-Peter-Lawwell-retire-Scottish-Rugbys-Dominic-McKay-replacement.html

[18] https://www.dailyrecord.co.uk/sport/football/football-news/eddie-howe-celtic-manager-announcement-24168260

[19] https://www.dailyrecord.co.uk/sport/football/football-news/eddie-howe-celtic-parkhead-manager-24206629

[20] https://www.dailyrecord.co.uk/sport/football/football-news/celtic-react-eddie-howe-bombshell-24207901

[21] https://www.dailyrecord.co.uk/sport/football/football-news/eddie-howe-odd-man-out-24335254
[22] https://www.67hailhail.com/news/celtic-announce-ange-postecoglou-as-manager/
[23] https://www.dailyrecord.co.uk/sport/football/football-news/neil-lennon-insists-inherited-celtic-24255247
[24] https://www.dailyrecord.co.uk/sport/football/football-news/neil-lennon-blasts-celtic-fans-24254543
[25] ibid
[26] https://twitter.com/Record_Sport/status/1401083561239793670
[27] https://twitter.com/celticfanzone/status/1401130393886199813
[28] https://thecelticblog.com/2021/05/articles-and-features/the-need-for-celtics-board-to-recapitalise-the-club/
[29] https://www.dailyrecord.co.uk/sport/football/football-news/celtic-take-aim-rangers-chief-23650984
[30] ibid
[31] https://www.glasgowtimes.co.uk/news/19149375.celtic-renewed-old-firm-trademark-rangers-days-were-not-half-anything-tweet/
[32] https://www.rangersnews.uk/news/celtics-old-firm-tweet-on-rangers-proved-wrong-by-official-gov-trademark/
[33] https://thecelticblog.com/2021/03/articles-and-features/celtic-has-put-our-questions-over-the-old-firm-trademark-issue-to-bed/
[34] Ibid

Chapter 5

[1] https://www.dailyrecord.co.uk/sport/football/football-news/steven-gerrards-rangers-anger-john-23604461
[2] https://thecelticblog.com/2021/03/the-ibrox-operation/police-scotland-ignored-the-law-at-livingston-they-better-step-up-their-game/
[3] https://thecelticblog.com/2021/03/the-ibrox-operation/scalpings-stunts-and-stupid-peepul-sevconias-triumph-is-already-farcical/7/#gallery-slide
[4] https://thecelticblog.com/2021/03/the-ibrox-operation/police-scotland-ignored-the-law-at-livingston-they-better-step-up-their-game/
[5] https://www.dailyrecord.co.uk/news/scottish-news/man-filmed-performing-sex-act-23624582
[6] https://www.dailyrecord.co.uk/news/scottish-news/rangers-fans-marched-away-ibrox-23624784
[7] https://twitter.com/ArtyBagger/status/1368656446913708035
[8] https://www.dailyrecord.co.uk/news/scottish-news/celtic-shop-vandalised-amid-chaotic-23627611
[9] https://www.dailyrecord.co.uk/news/scottish-news/police-arrest-28-people-rangers-23627055
[10] ibid
[11] https://www.dailyrecord.co.uk/news/scottish-news/rangers-fans-leave-huge-piles-23626816
[12] https://www.glasgowlive.co.uk/news/glasgow-news/george-square-

memorial-benches-vandalised-19987808
[13] https://www.dailyrecord.co.uk/news/scottish-news/rangers-fans-raise-thousands-pounds-23629873
[14] https://www.dailyrecord.co.uk/sport/football/football-news/celtic-fans-no-right-condemn-23663660
[15] https://twitter.com/SamAnth0ny/status/1369285263801876484
[16] https://www.dailyrecord.co.uk/news/scottish-news/rangers-contributed-disgraceful-title-party-23730444
[17] https://twitter.com/michaelmcp/status/1368637924040990727
[18] https://www.dailyrecord.co.uk/news/politics/rangers-write-nicola-sturgeon-first-23641212
[19] https://www.dailyrecord.co.uk/news/politics/rangers-fans-test-positive-coronavirus-23725298
[20] https://www.dailyrecord.co.uk/news/politics/rangers-fans-told-test-small-23734060
[21] https://thecelticblog.com/2021/05/the-ibrox-operation/ibroxs-fans-are-planning-to-break-the-law-police-scotland-cant-ignore-that/
[22] https://twitter.com/heyheyadaibhi/status/1368710740190900232
[23] https://twitter.com/noapologists69/status/1391305267711729665
[24] ibid
[25] https://www.followfollow.com/forum/threads/on-this-day-in-2008-rangers-took-over-manchester-as-over-200-000-fans-travelled-for-the-uefa-cup-final-against-zenit.164391/
[26] https://www.dailyrecord.co.uk/sport/football/football-news/rangers-fans-decorate-george-square-24103916
[27] https://www.followfollow.com/forum/threads/the-flags-are-up-in-george-sq.164345/
[28] https://www.dailyrecord.co.uk/news/scottish-news/rangers-fan-severely-injured-after-24147461
[29] https://www.gofundme.com/f/get-gary-back-up-the-ladders?utm_source=customer&utm_medium=copy_link_all&utm_campaign=p_cp+share-sheet
[30] https://www.followfollow.com/forum/threads/the-flags-are-up-in-george-sq.164345/
[31] https://www.followfollow.com/forum/threads/rangers%E2%80%99-union-bears-fans-group-put-up-anti-snp-and-anti-independence-banners-as-election-day-begins.163626/
[32] https://www.dailyrecord.co.uk/news/scottish-news/hundreds-rangers-fans-arrive-northern-24115080
[33] https://www.bbc.co.uk/sport/football/57102181
[34] https://www.dailyrecord.co.uk/sport/football/football-news/steven-gerrard-greets-jubilant-rangers-24114912
[35] https://www.dailyrecord.co.uk/news/scottish-news/cops-tell-rangers-fans-disperse-24115369
[36] https://www.dailyrecord.co.uk/sport/football/football-news/rangers-safety-breach-forces-sky-24116214
[37] https://thehoopsetter.wordpress.com/

[38] https://www.dailyrecord.co.uk/news/scottish-news/taxpayers-left-58-000-bill-24181943
[39] https://www.thescottishsun.co.uk/news/scottish-news/7127546/rangers-fans-george-square-paramedic-abuse-clyde-superscoreboard/
[40] https://www.dailyrecord.co.uk/news/scottish-news/scots-block-glasgow-immigration-raid-24099998
[41] https://www.bbc.co.uk/news/uk-scotland-glasgow-west-57136632
[42] https://www.thenational.scot/news/19303006.murdo-fraser-fire-irresponsible-tweet-rangers-fan-gatherings/
[43] https://www.thescottishsun.co.uk/news/scottish-news/7162422/rangers-fans-george-square-glasgow-damage-council-bill/
[44] https://www.msn.com/en-gb/news/newsscotland/hundreds-of-loyalists-gather-at-glasgows-george-square-to-protect-cenotaph-from-vandalism-attacks/ar-BB15qGUq
[45] https://www.dailyrecord.co.uk/news/scottish-news/shocking-glasgow-brawl-sees-thugs-24117883
[46] https://www.dailyrecord.co.uk/news/scottish-news/glasgow-police-officers-left-broken-24121450
[47] https://www.dailyrecord.co.uk/news/scottish-news/cops-using-powers-disperse-rangers-24118174
[48] https://www.sundaypost.com/fp/police-warn-of-many-more-arrests-over-disorder-during-rangers-celebrations/
[49] https://www.dailyrecord.co.uk/news/scottish-news/scottish-cup-final-warning-cops-24156131
[50] https://www.dailyrecord.co.uk/news/scottish-news/duty-police-officer-fined-after-24152921
[51] https://www.rangers.co.uk/Article/club-statement-170521/6AyO7pBSz9X70zSnrvuFk4
[52] https://www.dailyrecord.co.uk/sport/football/football-news/rangers-plans-ibrox-party-revealed-24136768
[53] https://twitter.com/MTSMFTFTFJ/status/1393860976697647106
[54] https://twitter.com/lfmunro/status/1393986764017184773
[55] https://www.dailyrecord.co.uk/news/politics/john-swinney-rages-rangers-fans-24122557
[56] https://www.dailyrecord.co.uk/news/scottish-news/nicola-sturgeon-utterly-disgusted-rangers-24119584
[57] https://thecelticstar.com/at-long-last-the-truth-speaks-its-name-anti-catholic-bigotry-jim-spence-on-scotlands-shame/
[58] https://tfn.scot/news/charity-speaks-out-on-anti-irish-racism-after-rangers-title-win
[59] https://www.glasgowtimes.co.uk/news/19323420.amp/?ref=twtrec&__twitter_impression=true
[60] https://www.dailyrecord.co.uk/news/scottish-news/rangers-legend-mark-walters-darts-24160684
[61] https://twitter.com/BjCruickshank/status/1397340181313859584
[62] https://www.dailyrecord.co.uk/sport/football/football-news/mo-johnston-signed-rangers-how-11839877

[63] https://twitter.com/Hahahasevco1/status/1397846972887928834
[64] https://www.youtube.com/watch?v=xZweLtjNxZY
[65] https://www.youtube.com/watch?v=YCPhprR8CuU
[66] https://www.youtube.com/watch?v=jV1Qyx2s1JI
[67] https://twitter.com/Wass2020/status/1396401421554225155
[68] https://www.scotsman.com/news/opinion/columnists/rangers-campaign-to-turn-club-and-its-fans-into-social-pariahs-ignores-plight-of-young-working-class-white-males-john-mclellan-3246016
[69] ibid
[70] ibid
[71] https://twitter.com/GrahamSpiers/status/1393875284278104067
[72] https://www.followfollow.com/forum/threads/the-snp-rangers-community-and-parallels-with-other-countries-a-warning-from-history.165296/
[73] ibid
[74] https://twitter.com/Richiestoke/status/1397333398729994243
[75] https://www.dailyrecord.co.uk/sport/football/football-news/rangers-rightly-stood-up-racism-24164301
[76] https://www.youtube.com/watch?v=d2q2FFumob4
[77] https://www.dailyrecord.co.uk/news/scottish-news/footage-rangers-players-allegedly-singing-24124010
[78] https://www.thescottishsun.co.uk/sport/football/7125087/rangers-players-video-sectarian-pope/
[79] https://www.youtube.com/watch?v=5vIH13byabY
[80] https://www.dailyrecord.co.uk/news/scottish-news/rangers-players-alleged-sectarian-singing-24159044
[81] https://www.rangers.co.uk/Article/club-statement-210521/3QVwERdF4P6Ty6NjCkL0kL
[82] https://www.dailyrecord.co.uk/news/scottish-news/calls-humza-yousaf-apologise-rangers-24161054
[83] https://www.dailyrecord.co.uk/news/scottish-news/rangers-fans-petition-calling-humza-24162966
[84] https://www.thescottishsun.co.uk/news/scottish-news/7152713/humza-yousaf-rangers-video-police/
[85] https://twitter.com/murdo_fraser/status/1396395128122642437
[86] https://twitter.com/FollowRangersPR/status/1396792016663728137
[87] https://www.justgiving.com/crowdfunding/follow-rangers?utm_term=e56q9aqB2
[88] https://www.heraldscotland.com/news/19337877.facts-back-claims-scotland-sectarian-anti-catholic-bias/ The full article can be read here: https://scottishdailypost.co.uk/do-the-facts-back-up-claims-that-scotland-is-sectarian-with-an-anti-catholic-bias/
[89] https://twitter.com/AngelaHaggerty/status/1401458252228042752
[90] https://www.dailyrecord.co.uk/news/scottish-news/rangers-players-title-party-video-24398475
[91] https://www.dailyrecord.co.uk/entertainment/celebrity/line-dutys-martin-compstons-brilliant-24257064

Chapter 6

[1] https://www.hurriyetdailynews.com/galatasaray-confirms-case-of-covid-19-154778
[2] https://turkishpress.com/3-more-galatasaray-players-test-positive-for-covid-19/
[3] https://www.dailyrecord.co.uk/sport/football/football-news/rangers-europa-league-boost-galatasaray-22764640
[4] https://www.skysports.com/football/news/11959/12110062/rangers-standard-liege-missing-at-least-three-for-europa-league-clash-due-to-coronavirus
[5] https://www.dailyrecord.co.uk/sport/football/football-news/benficas-rangers-injury-crisis-deepens-23040834
[6] https://www.uefa.com/insideuefa/about-uefa/news/0260-100e8be7e01f-060e38b54b98-1000--synlab-to-provide-covid-19-testing-at-uefa-competition-matches/
[7] https://www.bbc.co.uk/sport/football/56054515
[8] https://www.bbc.co.uk/sport/football/56138759
[9] https://www.bbc.co.uk/sport/football/56259324
[10] https://www.bbc.co.uk/sport/football/56375487
[11] ibid
[12] https://www.youtube.com/watch?v=6Y1Uh0Y0qNw
[13] https://www.youtube.com/watch?v=JLXOKOUD2HY
[14] https://www.youtube.com/watch?v=ly7wLtLNyH8
[15] https://twitter.com/PaisleySteelman/status/1372667203795968000
[16] https://www.youtube.com/watch?v=v5DN-pQ88K4
[17] https://theathletic.com/news/glen-kamara-racist-abuse-rangers/DvDAPiCxwsfz
[18] https://www.youtube.com/watch?v=v5DN-pQ88K4
[19] https://www.glasgowlive.co.uk/sport/football/football-news/slavia-prague-racism-row-defender-20210605
[20] https://www.youtube.com/watch?v=ly7wLtLNyH8
[21] https://www.dailyrecord.co.uk/sport/football/football-news/slavia-prague-launch-astonishing-rangers-23828651
[22] https://www.thescottishsun.co.uk/sport/football/7125087/rangers-players-video-sectarian-pope/
[23] https://www.rangersnews.uk/news/rangers-fans-call-out-commentator-agenda-over-gers-star-who-cant-win/
[24] https://www.followfollow.com/forum/threads/steven-gerrard-calls-out-sfa-as-rangers-boss-hits-out-at-disciplinary-process-after-alfredo-morelos-ban.151310/
[25] https://www.dailyrecord.co.uk/sport/football/football-news/slavia-prague-launch-astonishing-rangers-23828651
[26] https://www.dailyrecord.co.uk/sport/football/football-news/rangers-racism-accused-ondrej-kudela-23825052
[27] https://www.thesun.co.uk/sport/football/14393448/slavia-prague-keeper-

fractured-skull-rangers-roofe/
[28]https://www.heraldscotland.com/sport/19292673.uefa-dismiss-rangers-appeal-four-game-kemar-roofe-ban-dangerous-assault/
[29] https://www.youtube.com/watch?v=u_BNbXbjXx0
[30]https://www.dailyrecord.co.uk/sport/football/football-news/michael-stewart-glen-kamara-racism-23763408
[31] ibid
[32]https://www.heraldscotland.com/sport/19037847.sfa-drop-charge-ross-county-player-michael-gardyne-abusing-rangers-striker-alfredo-morelos/
[33]https://www.rangersnews.uk/news/rangers-fans-slam-bbc-pundit-for-deplorable-take-on-kamara-incident/
[34]https://www.footballtransfertavern.com/rangers-fc-news/rangers-gers-ibrox-steven-gerrard-club-1872-michael-stewart-glen-kamara-ondrej-kudela/
[35]https://www.sowetanlive.co.za/sport/soccer/2021-03-20-bongani-zungu-supports-rangers-teammate-glen-kamara-in-racial-abuse-row/
[36] https://www.youtube.com/watch?v=xQYxv10_vrw
[37]https://www.rangers.co.uk/Article/in-full-steven-gerrards-slavia-prague-press-conference/5cHxckfMsU3SdBUiikSs9X
[38]https://www.thescottishsun.co.uk/sport/football/6847794/rangers-kamara-reveals-kudela-said-vile-racist-abuse/
[39]https://theathletic.com/news/glen-kamara-racist-abuse-rangers/DvDAPiCxwsfz
[40] https://www.bbc.co.uk/sport/football/56460653.amp
[41]https://www.msn.com/en-gb/sport/news/the-moment-rangers-players-reacted-with-fury-toward-michael-gardyne-amid-serious-comment-allegations/ar-BB1bGlpo
[42]https://www.thescottishsun.co.uk/sport/football/6847794/rangers-kamara-reveals-kudela-said-vile-racist-abuse/
[43]https://www.scotsman.com/sport/football/rangers/what-was-said-to-glen-kamara-rangers-player-accuses-slavia-pragues-ondrej-kudela-of-racism-gerrards-response-3171444
[44]https://www.dailyrecord.co.uk/news/scottish-news/rangers-glen-kamara-lawyer-aamer-23943510
[45]https://www.dailyrecord.co.uk/sport/football/football-news/slavia-prague-ultras-sick-glen-23763484
[46] https://www.youtube.com/watch?v=V10Zv-EQJyk
[47]https://www.dailyrecord.co.uk/news/scottish-news/sacked-rangers-kitman-claims-racism-23766356
[48]https://www.followfollow.com/forum/threads/sunday-mail-front-page.158948/
[49]https://www.dailyrecord.co.uk/sport/football/football-news/alfredo-morelos-agent-brands-rangers-23603178
[50]https://www.followfollow.com/forum/threads/sunday-mail-front-page.158948/page-3
[51]https://www.followfollow.com/forum/threads/sunday-mail-front-page.158948/
[52]https://www.dailymail.co.uk/sport/football/article-8289239/Luis-Suarez-

racially-abusing-Patrice-Evra-remains-one-Premier-Leagues-shameful-moments.html
[53] ibid
[54] https://thecelticblog.com/2021/03/articles-and-features/ibrox-rocked-by-new-racism-claims-even-as-scotland-rallies-round-kamara/
[55] https://www.dailyrecord.co.uk/sport/football/football-news/nicolae-stanciu-reignites-rangers-race-24262137
[56] https://www.skysports.com/football/news/11781/12252554/celtic-vs-rangers-glen-kamara-starts-for-steven-gerrards-side-as-players-choose-not-to-take-a-knee
[57] https://www.thescottishsun.co.uk/sport/football/6849816/dundee-united-stand-rangers-kamara-motherwell-stop-knee/
[58] https://www.bbc.co.uk/sport/football/56460653.amp
[59] https://www.thescottishsun.co.uk/sport/football/5829376/rangers-goldson-hurt-blm-social-media/
[60] https://www.thescottishsun.co.uk/sport/football/5828595/rangers-connor-goldson-black-lives-matter-instagram/
[61] https://www.thescottishsun.co.uk/sport/football/5831695/rangers-robertson-knee-not-welcome/
[62] https://www.thescottishsun.co.uk/sport/football/5829376/rangers-goldson-hurt-blm-social-media/
[63] ibid
[64] https://www.thescottishsun.co.uk/sport/football/4638380/rangers-uefa-ibrox-closed-section-racist-behaviour/
[65] https://twitter.com/deejaypb/status/1394210109014822912
[66] https://www.dailyrecord.co.uk/news/scottish-news/woman-charged-over-alleged-racist-24219532
[67] https://twitter.com/quadtreble/status/1394389516593647621
[68] https://www.dailymail.co.uk/news/article-2481474/EDLs-Muslim-member-fined-threatening-behaviour-Asian-men-rally.html
[69] https://metro.co.uk/2021/06/13/england-vs-croatia-fans-at-wembley-boo-players-taking-the-knee-but-drowned-out-by-applause-14763893/
[70] https://www.independent.co.uk/sport/football/england-euro-2020-knee-booing-b1860260.html
[71] https://www.glasgowtimes.co.uk/sport/19365983.scotland-decided-not-take-knee-euros/
[72] http://www.jeffholmes.co.uk/
[73] https://www.dailyrecord.co.uk/sport/football/football-news/three-reasons-rangers-fans-fallen-24270557
[74] ibid
[75] https://www.independent.co.uk/news/soccer-player-jailed-for-foul-play-1577101.html
[76] https://www.dailyrecord.co.uk/sport/football/football-news/three-reasons-rangers-fans-fallen-24270557
[77] https://www.followfollow.com/forum/threads/the-three-reasons-rangers-fans-have-fallen-out-of-love-with-the-scotland-national-team.167205/
[78] ibid

[79] https://inews.co.uk/sport/football/scotland-squad-euro-2020-full-team-announcement-line-up-fixtures-1008920
[80] https://www.msn.com/en-gb/sport/american-football/argentinian-ref-takes-knee-before-scotlands-match-but-no-players-do/ar-AALkd0t?ocid=uxbndlbing
[81] https://www.dailymail.co.uk/sport/sportsnews/article-9668523/Euro-2020-Croatia-NOT-knee-Wembley-ahead-opening-game-against-England-Sunday.html
[82] https://www.skysports.com/football/news/11095/12330282/scotland-to-take-a-knee-alongside-england-at-wembley-euro-2020-encounter
[83] https://www.mirror.co.uk/sport/football/news/glen-kamara-statement-racist-abuse-23762625
[84] https://www.bbc.co.uk/sport/football/56789585
[85] https://twitter.com/Pmacgiollabhain/status/1386736568296263680
[86] https://thecelticblog.com/2021/04/articles-and-features/parliamentarian-attempts-to-drag-celtic-into-the-weekends-ibrox-outrage/
[87] https://www.thescottishsun.co.uk/sport/football/7021673/zander-clark-rangers-daft-brother-hilarious-swipe-stjohnstone/
[88] https://www.weareperth.co.uk/wapforum/index.php?/topic/28556-zander/page/12/
[89] https://www.glasgowlive.co.uk/sport/football/football-news/alleged-homophobic-slur-aimed-rangers-19416686

Chapter 7

[1] https://www.myweddinganniversary.com/anniversaries/55th-year-anniversary/
[2] https://www.followfollow.com/forum/threads/what-does-55-this-season-mean-to-you.130758/
[3] ibid
[4] ibid
[5] https://twitter.com/RangersFC/status/1407337610461302791
[6] https://tickets.rangers.co.uk/PagesPublic/ProductBrowse/ProductTravel.aspx?ProductSubType=TOUR&FilterTemplate=TEMPLATE1
[7] ibid
[8] https://www.followfollow.com/forum/threads/rangers-trophy-tour-2021.168007/
[9] ibid
[10] https://tickets.rangers.co.uk/PagesPublic/ProductBrowse/ProductTravel.aspx?ProductSubType=TOUR&FilterTemplate=TEMPLATE1
[11] https://www.dailyrecord.co.uk/news/scottish-news/cadbury-launch-new-rangers-55-23831159
[12] https://www.rangers.co.uk/official-champions-products/38ucCkyw6lKhRhSdqcQNcB
[13] https://www.followfollow.com/forum/threads/dairy-milk-rangers-champions-bar.157576/
[14] https://www.dailyrecord.co.uk/news/scottish-news/cadbury-launch-new-

rangers-55-23831159
[15]https://www.dailyrecord.co.uk/news/scottish-news/fan-fuming-after-8-rangers-23935346
[16] ibid
[17]https://www.ebay.co.uk/itm/234049800186?chn=ps&norover=1&mkevt=1&mkrid=7101533165274578&mkcid=2&itemid=234049800186&targetid=4584826055637459&device=c&mktype=&googleloc=&poi=&campaignid=412354546&mkgroupid=1299623041023876&rlsatarget=pla-4584826055637459&abcId=9300541&merchantid=87779&msclkid=f8f103aa567b16f173c8637767811b56
[18]https://www.mirror.co.uk/sport/football/news/30-most-successful-football-clubs-19428893
[19]https://www.mirror.co.uk/sport/football/news/30-most-successful-football-clubs-19428893#comments-wrapper
[20] https://en.wikipedia.org/wiki/Al_Ahly_SC
[21]https://www.dailystar.co.uk/sport/football/top-15-most-successful-clubs-22480565
[22]https://www.sportbible.com/football/news-top-10s-rangers-headline-top-10-european-teams-with-most-league-title-wins-20210308
[23]https://www.soccerladuma.co.za/news/articles/international/categories/world-news/the-10-clubs-with-the-most-league-titles-worldwide/660141?gallery=660141&gallery-page=9#ig-660141
[24] https://www.linfieldfc.com/index.aspx
[25] https://www.linfieldfc.com/history.aspx
[26] https://www.followfollow.com/forum/threads/linfield-54-titles.123260/
[27]https://www.glasgowlive.co.uk/sport/rangers-vice-chairman-john-bennett-20960902
[28] ibid
[29]https://www.change.org/p/sfa-remove-sfa-compliance-officer-andrew-phillips-from-his-position

Chapter 8

[1]https://www.dailyrecord.co.uk/sport/football/football-news/dave-king-delivers-rangers-fan-24503841
[2] ibid
[3]https://onefootball.com/en/news/club-1872-complete-first-rangers-share-purchase-from-dave-king-32111248
[4]https://www.glasgowtimes.co.uk/news/19244777.club-1872-increase-rangers-stake-ibrox-share-deal/
[5]https://philmacgiollabhain.ie/2021/07/12/daves-shares-and-a-man-of-the-cloth/
[6]https://onefootball.com/en/news/club-1872-complete-first-rangers-share-purchase-from-dave-king-32111248
[7]https://www.dailyrecord.co.uk/sport/football/football-news/dave-king-delivers-rangers-fan-24503841
[8]https://www.glasgowtimes.co.uk/sport/15286948.craig-houston-steps-

down-from-the-board-of-rangers-fan-organisation-club-1872/
[9]https://www.thescottishsun.co.uk/sport/football/6051001/two-directors-rangers-club-1872-resign-explanation/
[10] Pat Anderson – Up To Our Knees: Anti-Catholic Bigotry in Scotland Chapter 11
[11]https://www.followfollow.com/forum/threads/two-club-1872-directors-have-reisgned.133473/
[12] ibid
[13]https://www.followfollow.com/forum/threads/just-noticed-club-1872-are-having-elections.165283/
[14]https://www.followfollow.com/forum/threads/the-letter-from-rev-stuart-macquarrie-which-prompted-me-to-stand-for-club-1872.166064/
[15] https://club1872.co.uk/about/board/
[16]https://www.followfollow.com/forum/threads/i-have-been-barred-from-standing-in-the-elections-for-club-1872.166049/
[17] ibid
[18] ibid
[19] ibid
[20] ibid
[21]https://www.followfollow.com/forum/threads/some-facts-surrounding-club-1872.169997/
[22]https://www.footballtransfertavern.com/rangers-fc-news/rangers-gers-ibrox-steven-gerrard-club-1872-stuart-mcquarrie/
[23]https://www.followfollow.com/forum/threads/general-meeting-club-1872.167279/page-16
[24]https://www.thescottishsun.co.uk/sport/football/6385621/rangers-fan-group-club-1872-salary-fawkes-king/
[25] ibid
[26] Pat Anderson – Clash Of The Agnivores – The Big Lie and its Consequences
[27]https://www.glasgowtimes.co.uk/news/19356174.former-rangers-director-malcolm-murray-stands-club-1872-board-election/
[28] Pat Anderson – Clash Of The Agnivores – The Big Lie and its Consequences
[29]https://www.glasgowtimes.co.uk/sport/19382679.rangers-club-1872-announce-board-election-results/
[30] https://club1872.co.uk/news/club-1872-share-purchase-announcement-2/
[31]https://www.thescottishsun.co.uk/sport/football/6051001/two-directors-rangers-club-1872-resign-explanation/
[32]https://www.glasgowtimes.co.uk/news/19356174.former-rangers-director-malcolm-murray-stands-club-1872-board-election/
[33] https://www.followfollow.com/forum/threads/my-gers.170373/
[34] ibid
[35] https://www.rangers.co.uk/mygers/3jvwIFGlkkLQkwaie3nYLl
[36]https://www.footballtransfertavern.com/rangers-fc-news/rangers-gers-ibrox-steven-gerrard-season-tickets-sold-out-premiership-mygers/
[37] Ibid

Chapter 9

[1] https://www.dailyrecord.co.uk/sport/football/football-transfer-news/alfredo-morelos-transfer-twist-rangers-24562056
[2] ibid
[3] https://en.wikipedia.org/wiki/2021_Copa_Am%C3%A9rica#Group_stage
[4] https://www.rangersnews.uk/international/alfredo-morelos-not-involved-as-colombia-crash-out-of-copa-america/
[5] https://www.ibroxnews.com/2021/07/12/rangers-looking-to-charge-25000-for-media-access/
[6] https://www.hitc.com/en-gb/2021/07/12/rangers-25k-charge-for-media-access-branded-worrying-by-english-media-outlet/
[7] https://www.dailyrecord.co.uk/sport/football/football-news/celtic-fan-conspiracies-rangers-cash-24452811
[8] https://www.talkceltic.net/forums/threads/hugh-keevins-banned-from-celtic-park.112033/
[9] https://www.followfollow.com/forum/threads/breakdown-of-the-fees-for-press-access.170161/
[10] ibid
[11] ibid
[12] ibid
[13] https://www.rangersnews.uk/club-news/rangers-fans-fume-as-loyal-photographer-willie-vass-priced-out-of-ibrox/
[14] https://www.footballtransfertavern.com/rangers-fc-news/rangers-gers-ibrox-steven-gerrard-willie-vass-arsenal/
[15] https://www.willievass.com/gallery-list
[16] http://www.londonfreelance.org/feesguide/index.php?&section=Photography&subsect=National+newspapers
[17] https://www.celticfc.com/news/2021/july/A-dominant-display-against-Bristol-City-ends-goalless/
[18] https://www.celticfc.com/news/2021/july/Celts-pay-the-penalty-as-Preston-win-pre-season-clash/
[19] https://www.celticfc.com/news/2021/july/Celtic-lose-out-to-West-Ham-United-at-Paradise/
[20] https://www.dailyrecord.co.uk/sport/football/football-news/celtic-vs-west-ham-live-24607601
[21] https://www.rangers.co.uk/article/report-gers-continue-preseason-against-tranmere/24YFcaG2gxVQyufm3rQCSx
[22] https://www.dailyrecord.co.uk/sport/football/football-match-reports/3-talking-points-rangers-prove-24614050
[23] https://www.rangers.co.uk/article/report-rangers-celebrate-150-years-with-a-win-over-real-madrid/5vJA7e9FUJCwF3VxvXH4EQ
[24] https://www.celticfc.com/news/2021/july/Celtic-delighted-to-sign-highly-rated-midfielder-Liel-Abada/
[25] https://www.bbc.co.uk/sport/football/57855563
[26] https://planetradio.co.uk/clyde/sport/football-news/celtic-champions-league-squad/

[27] https://twitter.com/AndrewMaclean_/status/1417848520153915395
[28] https://www.dailyrecord.co.uk/sport/football/football-news/liel-abada-celtic-champions-league-24586578
[29] https://www.dailyrecord.co.uk/sport/football/football-news/furious-rangers-hit-out-over-24588323
[30] ibid
[31] https://www.followfollow.com/forum/threads/furious-rangers-hit-out-over-celtic-fan-allocation-as-ibrox-side-claim-councils-decision-doesnt-make-sense.170898/
[32] ibid
[33] ibid
[34] https://www.dailyrecord.co.uk/sport/football/football-news/furious-rangers-hit-out-over-24588323

Chapter 10

[1] https://rangers.blue2web.co.uk/club/investor-centre/
[2] https://castore.com/blogs/press/castore-and-newcastle-united-fc-sign-landmark-multi-year-agreement
[3] https://www.chroniclelive.co.uk/sport/football/football-news/newcastle-united-agree-5million-year-19193551
[4] https://www.theguardian.com/football/2021/jul/12/fa-condemns-racist-abuse-england-players-social-media-euro-2020-final?fbclid=IwAR3aOj3T25wZ49dbG8yewIvG4SzMAF36032jXE6lLREDm42V6EDkWOPb0OE
[5] https://skwawkbox.org/2021/07/13/breaking-england-teams-downing-st-reception-was-cancelled-because-players-refused-to-meet-johnson/
[6] https://www.followfollow.com/forum/threads/racist-abuse-of-england-players-marcus-rashford-jadon-sancho-bukayo-saka-condemned-by-boris-johnson-and-fa.170054/
[7] https://www.dailyrecord.co.uk/news/scottish-news/rangers-union-bears-threatened-cops-24515344
[8] ibid
[9] https://www.orthodoxconservatives.uk/articles/ulsterisation-scotland
[10] https://www.holyrood.com/comment/view,the-ulsterisation-of-scottish-politics-is-here-thanks-to-the-conservatives_13511.htm

Printed in Great Britain
by Amazon